W9-BNQ-692

DEATH OF THE CHEATING MAN

What Every Woman Must Know About Men Who Stray

DEATH OF THE CHEATING MAN

What Every Woman Must Know About Men Who Stray

MAXWELL BILLIEON

RAY J

SBI

SIMON & SCHUSTER / ATRIA / STREBOR BOOKS

NEW YORK LONDON TORONTO SYDNEY

STREBOR BOOKS INTERNATIONAL
SIMON & SCHUSTER / ATRIA

Strebor Books
P.O. Box 6505
Largo, MD 20792

This book is a work of nonfiction.

ISBN 978-1-59309-399-0

Cover styling and creative development by Maxwell Billieon for The Billieon Group
Cover design: www.mariondesigns.com
Cover photograph: © Keith Saunders/Marion Designs
Styling by Jason McGee for The Billieon Group (www.TheBillieonGroup.com)

Manufactured in the United States of America

Table of Contents

vii   Acknowledgments

PART I

3   Who I Am

7   Why I Wrote This Book: The Demise of the Human Family; Women are the New Men

11   A Letter to Women

17   The Origin of Cheating

19   The Culture of Cheating

21   What is Cheating Today?

25   Redefining Cheating and Monogamy

27   What is the New Monogamy?

31   A Cheater's Mind

35   The Different Types of Cheaters

39   No Color Lines

41   The New Cheating—Social Network Cheating

45   Lies Cheaters Tell

49   Five Myths Why Men Cheat

50   Five Myths Women Consider Cheating

51   The Difference Between a Cheater and a Player

55   Great Men Do Cheat

59   Battle of the Sexes

63   Tiger Woods: The Cheating Prophet

67   Why Do Powerful Men Cheat So Badly?

73   Let Them Eat Cake: The Study

77   The Consequences of Cheating

PART II

83 Conversations with a Cheating Man—The Opening

87 Conversation #1—The Gift and the Curse:
Why Men Cheat

93 The Re-Education of the Male

97 Conversation #2—Good Guy vs. Bad Boy

105 Conversation #3—The Wrong Day to Cheat

115 Six Virtues of the New Man

121 Conversation #4—Life Imitating Art

129 Conversation #5—Know Your Limitations

137 Learning How Not to Cheat

141 Conversation #6—How I Learned Not to Cheat

147 Conversation Finale—The New Man

153 Getting a Man Upgrade

PART III

163 The Real Destruction of Women

167 How Women Enable Cheating

173 The 30-Day Rule

177 The Nookie Opportunity

183 How to Spot a Cheater

186 Five Signs a Man is Cheating

187 Finding Out if a Man Can Be Faithful

189 How to Keep a Faithful Man Committed

195 How to Become First in a Man's Life

199 Pockets Over Pedigree

205 The Valentine's Day Massacre

213 The Truth About Freaks and Good Girls

217 Pulling a Yoko Ono

223 What Men Really Want in a Woman

241 About the Authors

245 Just the Facts: Q&A

247 Reader's Discussion Guide

Acknowledgments

MAXWELL BILLIEON

To my Father, thank you for giving me the core values that helped me to restore myself to the man that I was meant to be.

To my Mother, thank you for inspiring me to write and giving me your wisdom when I've needed it most.

I would also like to thank all of my family members for their love and support.

Thanks to The Billieon Group for being the best professional team any CEO could ask for.

Thanks to Ray J for being willing to make yourself an example for others.

Thanks to Zane, Charmaine and everyone at the Strebor family for helping me with the gift to showcase my vision.

Thanks to Judith Curr for your attention and support.

Thanks to Keith Saunders, Yona Deshommes, Jason McGee, and Curtis Bunn for the behind-the-scenes polish.

KC Hooks, thanks for being my friend and brother.

MVJ, I cannot even begin to say how much you've meant to my life in so many ways. Thank you for just being!

Special thanks to everyone at the entire Simon & Schuster and Atria family.

I could not write without having the support of the global community of writers, publishers, book clubs and retailers—may you all have success in continuing to provide books that the world needs.

I would also like to say thank you to the special few people who were a part of my life during the years when my consciousness was not at its best. It is because of you that I became a Thinking Man and discovered a new way to live. I am forever grateful for having you in my life.

RAY J

First, I would like to thank Maxwell Billieon for being my guide, teacher and brother on my journey to becoming a new man. Your principles and wisdom helped me to gain the balance that I needed and I am eternally grateful.

I especially want to say thank you to my family—you've always stood by me and I love you more than my words can ever express!

Special thanks to everyone who worked to make this book happen—Your support and belief in my growth has been a source of inspiration and it was a pleasure to work with you.

To all of my friends personally and professionally, thanks for always supporting me in my endeavors.

Lastly, I want to recognize the women who have been a huge part of my evolution as a man. I will never forget the impact you've had on my growth and I dedicate this to you.

PART I

Who I Am

—Maxwell Billieon

I grew up in Southern California, in a family immersed in social affairs, politics and entertainment. From as long as I could remember, there was always a man in my family, or extended family, who was involved in a high-profile gig.

I've been "fortunately unfortunate" enough to have men around me in the various offices of local government, as well as in Congress, the Senate, the State Assembly and even the Lieutenant Governor. Real-life, high-line guys that even worked with icons as high-brow as the Kennedys.

And on the flip-side, I also had family that played in Major League Baseball and the National Football League along with a cousin who managed celebrity athletes and entertainers.

All of these men were my role models and watching them excel throughout my youth showed me that I could achieve practically anything that I put my mind to. Their successes gave me the confidence to make it out of a community that did not offer me the educational system that I deserved and showed me that color is not the measure for success.

My access to them gave me knowledge and with it came direct exposure to many more powerful and famous men that taught me swagger and the ways of the world. And even though I didn't know it then, my exposure to them was an early education on how and why men cheat and why powerful men cheat so badly.

You could say that the men I saw growing up were my examples of what men are; or at least what I thought men were supposed to be. It was because of them that I've always had a certain expectancy of myself, that one day I would grow up and achieve as they had. And the one thing they had all achieved with their success was cheating. That experience was the precursor to what was to become my own lifestyle as a cheating man—one that spanned twenty years of straight infidelity.

That's what made me an expert on the subject of cheating; my "street credibility," if you will.

You see, as a young male, you don't really pick and choose the information you take from adults. Somehow you possess a strong desire to emulate them. So when the powerful men of high ranking that are close to you cheat, you can't help but automatically think that cheating comes along with the territory; especially because no average Joe is being outwardly or blatantly faithful.

I was also the only boy in the family. I was always taught by my mother to protect, assist and provide for her and my sisters. "That's what a man does," she would say. Consequently, I grew up with an understanding of how to service a woman's needs. That training aided me in gaining insight into the minds of women. And eventually I learned to use it to play them without getting caught.

I began cheating at the earliest age possible. In elementary school, as soon as I found an attraction to the opposite sex, I began to cheat on them. But there was never a time growing up when any man, including the men that I've mentioned, guided me in this conquest. It was simply there. And not only for me, but also for all of the young boys around me, and we couldn't explain why.

As I grew into a young man, my chosen profession of the entertainment business was a veritable breeding ground for cheating. It's well-known that show business offers up quite an assortment of beautiful women and with success in the business, comes success with them. No one appeared to be faithful, male or female, and I slid right into it.

When my business began to take me around the world, I learned that cheating was an international practice. I saw that men everywhere were cheating—Asia, Europe, South America...you name it and I saw it. I remember one time that a guy I was working with in Japan introduced me to his wife in the morning, and then his mistress at night. He literally called them by those intimate titles. Ignorantly, it was something that he was quite proud of and arrogantly believed that it made him more of a man. At that time I thought that was how the world was supposed to be—full of alpha males like me that were meant to conquer the world of women.

The problem wasn't that I enjoyed having women. What man doesn't want to have a beautiful and intelligent woman on his arm? It was that I *always* had them when I was in a committed relationship…it was almost like I kept a relationship on the side of my cheating, instead of the other way around. And even though I felt guilty, I didn't know how to stop.

One night, while on an international business trip, I found myself thinking about changing my life. I lay there for a while, tossing and turning in bed, wondering if it was actually possible for a man to change. It was then that I began to take account of the cheating I'd been involved in for years, and I was urged to get up and write it all down.

The more I wrote, the more that came to mind. I couldn't believe what I was seeing on paper. But what really shocked me the most about my feelings was that even with all of my cheating, I still didn't think that I'd had enough. What I didn't know then, but would later learn, is that it's usually like that for most cheating men. They can never get enough—it's the conquering that drives the urge for more and more.

Let me break it down so you can really understand me.

From the very first moment I experienced my first kiss, I wanted more of it—I can't explain the urge but if you've had your first kiss, then you probably know what I mean. My school didn't offer me any basic training on it, nor did I have any God-given skill to discern what I was feeling or how to handle it. As I matured in age and went on to college, there was no class to teach me any of the basics I needed to control that desire, or even that I *should* control it. Sure, there were classes for everything else to further develop my educational skills. And socially I had lessons for all sorts of sports and activities. But there was no class or lesson plan to teach me to "learn how not to cheat."

And there you have it. That's the problem in a nutshell. I was never taught "how not to cheat." Like me, all males need an education to build our skills to perform any task, and that includes the skill to be faithful. It took me many years to figure that out—from age ten to thirty, to be exact. But once I formed this realization, I was able to break the chains of cheating and become a 100 percent faithful man. And I've never looked back. In fact, I can't believe that I ever cheated. The guy that was inside of me is dead!

That's how the name for this book came about. I believe that any true change or evolution kills off the old behavioral patterns and habits, and in its place, leaves a new person. That's what I did: I killed off the old me simply by developing some very basic principles that somehow society has forgotten to teach its males. Once we learn them, cheating quickly becomes a thing of the past.

Throughout the world, most men are exactly like me; I'm speaking of those guys that cheat or have cheated. The commonality among us is simply that we cheat for one reason and one reason only...because we do not know how not to. Believe me when I tell you that it's truly that simple!

Why I Wrote This Book

Cheating can happen to anyone and it often does. Any woman can be cheated on, at anytime by any man. If you think that you can't be cheated on, ask Maria Shriver and you will quickly learn that everyone is susceptible to it. And although today both men and women cheat, I directed my attention specifically to male cheating because I believe that the core of cheating starts with men. If we stop, then women will stop.

"I'm not a reformed cheater; I am a reformed man!" I say that because once I learned the principles of "how not to cheat," my life changed overall. I became more responsible for my actions across the board and that gave me the ability to make better choices in relationships and life in general.

THE DEMISE OF THE HUMAN FAMILY

As you will soon read, there is much proof that male cheating has caused a huge increase in female cheating in the last decade. And that increase has contributed to a growing divorce rate that is at an all-time high. The consequence of this has meant a steady decline in new marriages, leaving the family structure, as we once knew it, in peril.

Now more than ever before, it is clear that men are in need of a new model to help us create faithful and committed relationships, or our cheating will surely be the cause of the demise of the human family at large.

WOMEN ARE THE NEW MEN

Throughout this book I make the statement that "Women are the new men." I say this because modern women are truly phenomenal. They have advanced well past the expectations and acceptance of men who for centuries placed them in second position. Their resilience has moved them through female-driven movements into a modern lifestyle of hunting alongside man.

Every day they head out into the world to conquer, bringing home food for their families, while man has hidden behind the antediluvian mentality that he is king of all. But gentlemen, if we listen closely we can hear the chants extolling, "the king is dead—long live the queen."

However, even with the success of women, they are not seeking to conquer men as we have done to them. Instead, they ask that we men become their partners in a new social structure; and although they do not yet have a working model of such a partnership, they are more than open to our suggestions and direction...their only demand is that we are faithful.

That is why I wrote this book. So that I could provide the model that both men and women should have to beat cheating. This book is for both the cheater and the person who has been or may be cheated on. It is an actual education on how not to cheat, as well as a guide on how cheating works, the different types of cheaters and how to prevent cheating from causing the demise of your family and life.

Part 1 is dedicated to giving you all of the background information you will need to truly understand what cheating is in today's world and why men are so consumed by it. We men are born conquerors.

Part II of the book is a guide to learning how we men can use that conqueror to kill the cheater inside of all of us. It is also a journey alongside one of the most notorious playboys of today's media-driven world. His life is a case study of how the principles of this book can change anyone.

As I have said, "Women are the new men," and are equally as important as men in this book, if not more, because cheating can only exist if women allow it to continue. That's a strong statement but women have more power than they've ever recognized in male cheating. Part III of this book will showcase how much power that truly is and what can be done with it to prevent cheating.

Finally, I'm not one of those people who is somehow thankful for their mistakes or sees them as something I needed to go through to make myself a better person. I have learned that consequence is the most important thing in life and the consequence of cheating is that it hurts and damages other people and I am remorseful to have ever taken part in it.

I believe that with remorse comes a responsibility to help others avoid making the same mistakes that I have made. That is my personal and professional goal—to help ensure that we can all contribute to putting an end to the deadly cycle of cheating, for once and for all.

I offer this book as an example of how, with a new model and education, men and women can finally reshape and enhance their lives to form fruitful and prosperous relationships for the future and I hope that you find it can work for you, as it has for me.

—Maxwell Billieon

A Letter to Women

What is insanity?

The great Albert Einstein said, "Insanity is doing the same thing over and over and expecting different results."

If this definition is accurate, then women are, scientifically speaking—INSANE!

This is obvious in the daily demonstrations of your expectations of men to be able to be monogamous. This single expectation has tormented women for centuries. The scary part is not that your insanity has not changed; it is that it has affected your own nature, forcing you to adopt man's insane ideals, methods and philosophies to survive in his jungle called infidelity.

"A sane person knows they're insane;" that's my philosophy. And because women haven't yet realized that they are insane, it is in their demand for a man's monogamy without educating him on how to be monogamous, that their insanity is showcased the most.

But women aren't alone in this insanity.

Monogamy and infidelity go hand in hand in the annals of man's long residence on this planet. A recent infidelity poll stated that 74 percent of men said they would cheat on their wives if they knew they couldn't get caught. This is not surprising because infidelity has remained the No. 1 cause of divorce in America and Europe since its earliest poll taken. And men represent more than half of the cases of reported cheating, according to a poll of American divorce lawyers.

There are literally millions of cases of cheating in global history. Most of them list men as the offender and many of those men have been of royal, political and social high-ranking.

Believe it or not, cheating is the largest cause of divorce in world history, evolving over generations and remaining as relative to the time in which we live today, as it did in centuries past.

What then is to be said about the sanity of man who for millenniums has continued cheating, while expecting women to remain forever faithful?

In this, he is also truly insane!

But wait, you can't blame men; our problem with cheating is not our fault. How could man have ever evolved past cheating without learning the principles that govern his inability to be monogamous? It is impossible!

I admit that it is time for men to stop cheating and evolve into responsible beings; or to accept that they are incapable of monogamy, choosing a truthful foundation in polyamory.

But in order for men to reach this level of consciousness, both men and women will have to become partners in the concept of "New Monogamy." That means the acceptance by women that every man isn't made for traditional monogamy and some men may want to have more than one partner until they are groomed for lasting one-on-one love.

If women don't learn to be more open to helping form this new monogamy, then it is them who will lose most of all; there are far less men than there are women. And that means men have more opportunities to find the right woman, than women have to find the right man.

I recently saw a male relationship therapist say on television that the most important element in today's families is whether or not a man is there for his children. He went on to add that whether a man is with the mother of his children or not is no longer important.

Can you believe that, ladies? This is how you're thought of in today's world. You are not considered to be important and have become second to everything and everyone; even though you now make the money and pay the bills. It doesn't matter; your monetary success doesn't mean you'll earn a good man, healthy relationship, or even respect.

It seems that no matter how hard women have tried to raise their level of respect with men, and women have tried hard for centuries, they cannot bypass being considered the secondary creature in the human-chain.

It's caused a battle between men and women. Men cheat, so women cheat…in fact, today 54 percent of women in committed relationships stated that they have cheated at least once, according to the poll by the American Divorce Lawyers. For men the percentage was 57 percent. The difference between the sexes is only 3 percent and that's un-freaking believable!

However, the light at the end of that tunnel is that it clearly demonstrates that women will work as hard as men, for better or worse; but now women have to work smarter.

Make no misake, ladies; this book is not some sort of slick outcry by a man to get women to stay at home, have more sex, or learn how to cook again. This is a guide to show everyone that the time has come for both sexes to evolve past cheating and learn a new model to have successful relationships.

But if all the stats weren't enough to convince you that I'm right, let's factor in race, because it also plays a role in the men that some women will date; especially women of color. Their numbers become even smaller as certain ethnicities restrict themselves to men of their own ethnic groups.

This is not to say that there is no man for you, ladies, but simply to bring you to the reality that for true happiness, your upward growth must include a loving relationship and to let you know that you can have that on your own terms. But to get that perfect man, it's not just men who have to stop cheating on you; you also have to stop cheating yourselves.

It's understandable that because you've had to take care of yourself, due to men's inability to grow at your pace, you have lost time and interest in traditional pursuits to form lasting relationships and have learned to cheat as much as men do. Personally, I can't blame you for learning to fight fire with fire or for stepping up to the plate in a man's absence to take care of your children. Someone had to do it and you've done it well.

But let's be completely honest, it takes "a real man" to complete a woman. Any woman who says that she doesn't need a man to complete her happiness is probably single. And although some women may not admit it publicly, there are enough examples now to show that without a good man in a woman's life, women are growing increasingly dissatisfied with the career successes that they have had to use to preoccupy themselves because of an inability to find a good man that doesn't cheat.

But I digress, why be with a man if he's gonna cheat on you? After all, you have proven that you can do fine all by yourself. It's true; you don't need a cheating man in your life and that's why we're here. So that you can finally count on a man to be faithful and make you better; not drive you insane with his cheating ways.

So if I can keep it real for a minute, let me as a man say that you no longer have to accept the philosophies of your foremothers and sisters that believed that they needed to bear the burden of having a cheating mate. They were wrong in their belief that you should accept a man's cheating and deal with it by settling for the man who is best at hiding his infidelities. That belief did not force or guide men into monogamy; it only served to encourage our cheating more.

You were once denied the right to vote and to be educated alongside men. Now you have become 50 percent of the corporate work force in America and control over 80 percent of household spending. It is obvious that you're strong, so use your strength to avoid becoming like men…the risks are too great and the consequence of your cheating means the destruction of our families.

You can take it from me because I was once a cheating man. A non-yielding and lie-wielding female distraction built on miseducation. A victim of misguided men who came millenniums before me; ignorant role models that I blindly followed to fulfill the desires of my nature.

But if I learned "how not to cheat," so will other men. The time has come where men like me realize that we need you for more than procreation, as we were taught was your purpose. We need you for partnership and to nurture us into communal health. After all, it's your nature to provide nurturing to those who have fallen.

Ladies, you are the only light in the darkness that man has created and you can't let that light go out!

So as a former cheater, I ask women to read this book with an open mind. I have lined its pages with the facts, cases, stories and anecdotes that are geared to help you better understand men and see what you can do to enhance your dating and relationship experience. It is my intention to guide us all to a new model of intimate success in hopes that we men will finally allow you to become what you were meant to be: a woman.

I've got your back, ladies, the New Man is here—I am the New Man!

The Origin of Cheating

*In the beginning, God created the heavens and the earth—
and cheating, too?*

Have you ever asked yourself what the actual origin of cheating was? Who was the first person to cheat and where did it take place? What if I told you that it happened in the Garden of Eden— would you believe me?

It is virtually impossible to examine the beginning of cheating without looking at it through the lens of popularized religion; only because that is where the majority of the world has learned the concept of creation. But in our search for man's beginnings, we may have been missing a very important element to our problem with relationships. If you really look at it, the story of creation doesn't merely carry the concept of the creation of man or time, but it also gives us the creation of his problem with cheating.

According to popular religious teachings, when God created the heaven and the earth, there was no sin, at least not on earth. And when God created Adam and Eve, sin still had not shown its face on earth.

It wasn't until Eve gave the apple to Adam that cheating began to surface; her intent was to betray God's command. Once Adam took a bite of the apple, cheating was fully born.

If you're still asking how that is cheating, let me explain further.

According to those teachings, God said that Adam and Eve had sinned against Him when they ate the apple. But after that God didn't provide them with a guide or an education on how to deal with the contradicting sexual emotions they'd face from their infamous bite. Instead, Adam was given the gift and curse of having a choice, and since that moment, man's inability to choose has been at the root of his confusion to be monogamous or to cheat.

That simply doesn't seem fair. Has man somehow been destined to cheat because God left us without an education on how not to?

If you believe the story, then it very well could be…isn't that the reason that monogamy was created in the first place?

Think about it; before there was sin, monogamy wasn't needed. Once sin came into the picture, monogamy became a necessary concept to keep things fair. In fact, before there was sin, man and woman would not have known the desire for a monogamous relationship. Freedom was built into the nature of our existence on earth and other than eating that apple, we were set up to live here without constriction.

Once the act of sin was realized, so was cheating. That means that the sin that Adam and Eve were charged with goes hand in hand with cheating. Another way to look at it is to picture sin and cheating as Siamese twins that serve as each other's life support and are never split.

It seems that men could have benefited from a lesson on how to deal with the desire to cheat around that time. With all due deference to religion, when we're confronted with the temptation of infidelity, asking ourselves "what would Jesus do" isn't enough to resist the natural inclination to cheat. Especially since the Bible teaches that Jesus never had a woman, clearly, cheating wouldn't have been His issue.

But maybe God's plan for us was to create a way to choose monogamy over cheating? Well, in case you still aren't sure, let's dig a little deeper.

Again, in the story of creation it states that when God put Adam and Eve in the Garden of Eden, He gave them rules to govern His relationship with them. They agreed to live by those rules and were wed to Him; by definition, that is called monogamy.

This meant that Adam and Eve were in a monogamous relationship with God and in respect of the rules of monogamy, when Adam and Eve bit the apple and listened to Satan, they cheated on God.

Therefore, the first sin ever committed was cheating.

The Culture of Cheating

Cheating: "A dishonest act in order to gain advantage"
(ENGLISH-AMERICAN DICTIONARY)

I consider cheating a culture because by definition, any social form of society that encompasses a set of beliefs and activities that are systematically practiced by a social establishment is a culture. Therefore, by sharing the values, perspectives, goals and practices of cheating, cheaters are a part of a culture—the culture of cheating.

There are many factors that have contributed to the formation of the cheating culture in our world today. For one, cheating does not observe or lend itself to race, class or ethnic origin. It invites all who are willing to integrate it into their lives.

And millions of people have done that. Without us even being aware, cheating has snuck its way into our mainstream social values; so much so that it has become normal and even expected to be a part of our relationships at some point and time.

It's not even a secret anymore! During our parents' era, if a man cheated, it was kept private and in the dark. Today, it is discussed openly on television, the Internet and in any popular setting without pause.

Yet as much as we see cheating on a regular basis, it still goes totally misunderstood by men and women. Women still believe that cheating is a fate that they are destined to endure, whether they like it or not, and men believe that it's the natural and intrinsic way we are wired to live. Both are extremely wrong.

If we look at cheating as being cultural, we see that it can be undone, like the general practices of any culture. We can also see that cheating itself is not the problem; it's merely a symptom of a lack of training, or the result of poor training. It's a symptom like the sore throat of a cold, but not the cold itself. And like with a cold, the key to ridding ourselves of this annoying sore throat is to eliminate the cold and our health gets restored.

To do that, we have to understand how cultures are formed. Generally, cultures are established on a foundation of systematic ideals and beliefs. Those ideals and beliefs govern the entire cultural establishment, including sex, relationships, education and societal disciplines. Every so often, a new set of ideals is introduced to the old thinking that totally shakes the foundation of the prior social establishment's cultural beliefs. Usually the more traditional members of the culture fight it. But as a new era and generation emerge, their new way of thinking takes over the old ideals. "Out with the old and in with the new." That is always the mantra of the next generation.

For our parents' generation, cheating was an act that was considered more of a male problem. But women have adopted an "if he can do it, so can I" mentality and, consequently, they are cheating almost as much as men; and it's getting out of control. So with both sexes cheating equally as much, we have a formed a new culture of cheating.

But women will not make the playing field level by cheating as much as men. That is only making the problem worse. And men can't continue to cheat without expecting women to do the same. To change the culture, we have to change the cultural ideal. That will require that both men and women change the way we perceive monogamy and infidelity. By understanding that our problems are not gender based, but they are simply the result of a lack of education, both men and women can change cheating from being a culture, to becoming an aberration.

What is Cheating Today?

There are so many opinions on what cheating is in today's modern society. How much intimate interaction with the opposite sex is actually cheating? And what's the limit that a man can go to before he's cheating when he's in a committed relationship?

Because opinions differ from person to person and especially from woman to woman, it's been impossible to come up with one universal ideal or definition of cheating. Today's relationships are more complex than those of previous generations. Many adults now feel that they can make their own rules to fit their particular relationship. For them, the concept of traditional monogamy is considered outdated and, in some cases, even looked down upon. The truth is that modern people simply no longer want to feel that they are confined to the same rules that governed their parents.

After millenniums of following the so-called "rules of monogamy," men and women now enter relationships with the desire to satisfy many of their individualistic needs, much in the same way as if they were single. Everyone seems to want his or her cake and ice cream, so to speak.

Although, now more than ever, there are women that allow men more leniency with innocent flirtations and non-traditional contact with other women, for most women, the rules of monogamy have remained traditional.

However, as modern as today's women are, when I interviewed many of them for this book to see how they defined cheating, I learned that there is one universal commonality among them all: that no matter what, any intimacy outside of the relationship is considered cheating.

In contrast, my research amongst men yielded completely different results. Men felt that there should be room to make up new rules in their relationships. For men, enjoying another woman's company outside of the relationship without physical intimacy is not always seen as cheating, and that is where the issue seems to become a serious problem.

Men and women still don't see eye to eye on what cheating is.

Ask a man if having a thought about another woman is cheating and almost 100 percent of them will say no. "That's taking it too far to me and sounds more like a woman that feels that way is really insecure," one of the guys I interviewed said.

"C'mon, it's ridiculous that in 2012 a man could be cheating

What Women See As Cheating

To put a bull's-eye on this issue, I asked ten women between the ages of twenty-one and forty what they considered cheating and here are their responses:

Watching porn

Going out with another woman (movies, dinner, events, etc.)

Kissing another woman

Having a secret female friend (without sex being involved)

Fantasizing about another woman (other women)

Flirting with women (without intent to go further)

Getting another woman's phone number or personal information

Having secret email conversations with another woman

Having chat room visitations with other women

Having phone sex with another woman

Visiting and viewing sex webcam sites

Talking to or maintaining contact with other women via a social networking site

by fantasizing about someone that he doesn't know and will never probably even meet, like a celebrity or model," another guy said.

Obviously, there are so many different ideas of what cheating is today that it's impossible to tell who is right and who is wrong. The truth is that we need to finally redefine what cheating is; otherwise, we will continue in this idealistic confusion.

But first, I wanted to showcase how extreme the differences are between men and women so I brought in a man whose lifestyle epitomized the modern-day cheater's perspective of idealistic machismo.

Ray J is a celebrity that many people have followed for years via music and television. He came to public consciousness as a very young man who was known for being as much of a charmer as he was a performer. And as he grew into manhood, he developed a serious penchant for getting multiple women of all shades, sizes and backgrounds. Eventually, his female escapades and womanizing took over and his playboy lifestyle became tabloid headlines all over the world as he bedded well-known video sirens, models, actresses, singers and reality-show stars, some of whom even became more famous after having intimate affairs with him.

But what most people don't know is that Ray J had always been a cheating man. After learning this, I decided to include him in the book as the perfect male case study of the modern cheating man. To gather as much information as possible, one of the first things I asked him was what he thought cheating was. And his answer showcased how wide the gap is between the male and female perspectives about the issue.

RAY J: Personally, I believe that cheating is when you lie to someone and lead them to believe that they are the only one. Especially if you say you will never-ever-ever have sex with another person. Cheating is about sex, right?

The problem is that with women, it gets more complex than that, even when you are up front with them.

It's like this, having one woman has always been difficult for me. I admit that I cheated on women but I also tried to keep it real and tell a woman from the onset that I wanted to be with other women. That way she understood that I was gonna do my thing, even if she wanted to be with me in a monogamous relationship. I didn't want the drama that came along with having her think that I was not gonna be a free spirit.

But after we got more intimate, she accused me of cheating when I was with someone else, even though I had told her what I wanted straight up. I couldn't win! No matter how I shaped it, she still felt that me being with someone else and with her was cheating.

So, eventually, I gave up and kept my business to myself. As much as I hate to say it, that seemed to make it a lot easier for me. It's true what they say; what they don't know won't hurt 'em!"

As I think back to our parents' era, cheating basically meant any physical contact outside of someone's own traditionally monogamous relationship. Back in the day, as long as a man took care of the family, women tended to close their eyes to infidelities. But now women require men to partner with them and that makes the playing field even.

Naturally, there are already many innate differences between men and women. In addition, religion, social standards and cultural and ethnic differences make a mosh pit of opinions that seem to slam-dance into one another.

So what exactly is the definition of cheating today? To redefine cheating we also have to redefine monogamy. By placing a definitive modern definition on both of these terms, we can create the consciousness and education that will keep both men and women from giving up on having successful relationships.

Redefining Cheating and Monogamy

Is traditional monogamy still a relevant concept for today's relationships? Few couples have ever been able to navigate it successfully and those that have, still complain about the amount of hard work that it takes to constantly observe the strict rules that traditional monogamy demands.

The problem for today's couples is that no one has ever gotten to participate in the rules of how monogamy governs their lives. We inherited the concept from our parents as they did from their parents. The rules were passed down to all of us and we had no choice but to accept them. That is, not until now...

As beautiful as it is when two people click, not everyone wants to have a traditional one-on-one relationship forever. Actually, some people would rather choose polyamory over monogamy and there's nothing wrong with that. If someone wants to keep their options open at all times, they should be free to do so without any pressure from society to conform.

But there are also people that do want to be with one person, but either can't or simply don't want to do it the old school way. They want to get married but struggle with it, because deep inside they feel they can't live up to its demanding rules. If possible, they'd rather be able to enjoy a relationship any way they see fit. That may include having intimate relationships and friendships with others. It may also mean the freedom to be flirtatious or maintain friendships with the opposite sex with no sexual attachment whatsoever. But these things aren't generally permitted by the traditional monogamous infrastructure. So for people with those desires, let me present to you what I am calling "The New Monogamy."

What is the New Monogamy?

"The breaking of any rule that governs a couple's intimate relationships or interactions with other people." — MAXWELL BILLIEON

L ike traditional monogamy, "NM" also means two people coming together in a committed relationship with one another. However, unlike traditional monogamy where a couple is forced to adhere to principles that they didn't create, NM provides them with the ability to make their own rules and implement whatever disciplines of monogamy are most comfortable for them as a unit.

To put it bluntly, whatever rules a couple decides to live under in their relationship today are okay. As long as both people consciously agree to them and respect the rules, they are living in monogamy—the New Monogamy.

PEOPLE MAKE THE WORLD GO ROUND

The world is made up of different people...we all have a plethora of different likes and dislikes. What works for one person may not work for someone else, so why should they both have to be committed under the same rules?

I personally know a couple that allows each other a hall pass once a year. I also know a pastor and his wife that would never think of such a thing (at least they say they won't). No one should ever feel guilty for being different, and as adults, we don't have to anymore.

Let's face it; relationships are difficult enough as it is; instilling a universal set of rules to govern every relationship the same way has never worked. Most of our parents and ancestors stayed married because divorce was shameful. Women stayed with unfaithful men because they wanted to keep their families together. But now the divorce rate is at an all-time high, so obviously, the days of staying married because it looks good are over!

Men and women have begun to accept new roles in society. It's time for relationships to get a makeover as well. To borrow a term from the fashion world, we can make personalized "Couture Relationships."

If you and your mate want something different, you don't have to restrict yourself to old school monogamy. Say that you are a modern-conservative who believes in maintaining some of the traditional principles. You and your mate can tailor those to fit your needs. Or if you and your mate like to get your freak on and want to have options, then more power to ya! After all, what you do with your mate is no one's business but yours.

I'm sure I'm not the only one who has noticed that traditional monogamy made everyone miserable. If it worked, we wouldn't have thousands of books that try to teach us how to do it successfully. It would be much more intrinsic in our wiring as men and women.

Sure, maybe there was a time when women wanted it, but now that they've tasted independence, they don't want to give it up.

But wait, before we get too far, let me say that I'm not suggesting that anyone force a mate that wants a traditional relationship to get into NM. Some people are more comfortable with keeping things the way that they've always been. If that works for them, then they should be able to do that as well.

That's exactly why we need a new concept of monogamy, so that each couple can design a set of principles that work without prejudice, disrespect or distrust.

This is about working to modernize the outdated concept of monogamy by allowing adults to act as exactly that—adults. So if you are one of the millions—no, billions—of people that struggle with the old school monogamy, then making your own personal New Monogamy is probably the thing for you.

RULES ARE FOR ADULTS

Let me be clear. New Monogamy isn't about having peripheral relationships outside of traditional monogamy. It is more so about each couple making new rules that enhance their individual and jointed goals for a healthy relationship.

Every relationship is different—we no longer live in a black and white world that requires us to all live by the same standards. Yet and still, every relationship needs rules to establish and maintain integrity. Without rules, you have assumption and anarchy simply because we don't all come from the exact same backgrounds.

Our differences in upbringing make problems in most male-female relationships; primarily because we naturally communicate very differently and we are never taught how to communicate with each other in relationships.

As humans, we naturally work better when the rules are laid out up front. Most people also want to feel like they are a part of forming any rule that would govern their lives. Consequently, relationships are more successful when we are involved in making the rules that govern us to ensure that our individual interests and needs are formed inside of the fabric of the relationship.

Making rules together is the only way we are truly prepared for the different obstacles that constantly confront relationships today.

HOW TO TAILOR YOUR OWN "COUTURE RELATIONSHIP"

Great communication is always the cornerstone of any successful relationship. It creates a platform for the relationship to stand on as challenges present themselves.

Tailoring the rules of a relationship for two people with rules that meet both of their needs requires great communication as well as acceptance. In order to attain or maintain healthy relationships, both people must feel like their individual needs are being met.

For anyone desiring to enter the New Monogamy, sitting down to communicate your individual needs openly and honestly is the first step.

Should we maintain relationships with the opposite sex and how much is too much? What are the parameters of those relationships and what's fair play or completely off limits? These issues need to be agreed to in order to ensure that there is no room for deception, disrespect or cheating.

Of course we will always need to compromise certain things when we commit to someone else. At the same time, it's equally important to accept that our mate's individual needs or requests aren't considered wrong or right; they are desires that each couple can reshape to fit their individual needs into prosperous ideals that are better suited for a jointed relationship.

So, if you've decided that you're ready for a real commitment, consider New Monogamy and you may find that it's the perfect fit for your lifestyle.

A Cheater's Mind

Inamed this chapter "A Cheater's Mind" because in comparison, the insanity of cheating men is uniquely similar to the mentality of the character in the Academy Award-winning film, *A Beautiful Mind*.

For anyone that doesn't know the story, the main character, John, is a brilliant mathematician turned professor who loses control of his mind early in life without realizing it. For years he lives in an alternate reality that is 100 percent real to him, never suspecting that he has gone insane.

As he matures, his ability to process and rationalize reality fades, and in its place, the alternate world takes over, and makes him functionally insane.

I believe that is the perfect example of men in our relationship with cheating today…we have been cheaters for so long, we have become functionally insane.

In the film, John's insanity grows and grows until his wife finally recognizes the signs. She immediately tries to get him to face it and attempts to show him that the people and voices he thinks he sees and hears aren't real. But, as is the normal male reaction, when we are told we our insane, he fights it and makes every argument that he is normal.

After battling back and forth, his wife seeks help and a psychologist prescribes a series of shock therapy sessions and medications to keep the man stable. It is hard-core and exhausting, to say the least. So once he is worn down, John finally accepts his condition.

But stubborn and determined to overcome his problem on his own, he turns away the therapy in belief that he can power his way through his condition with willpower, which of course, proves futile.

Again, that's exactly the same issue that men have with beating cheating. Even when we know we have a problem, we refuse to address it. And many of us believe that we have no choice but to accept that it's the way we are supposed to be. We let our egos convince us that we are strong enough to battle through it, only to lose to temptation every time.

The part of the film that shows the truest similarity to cheating is in the end. After so many years of battling against himself and failing, John finally fully accepts his issue head-on. He develops the understanding that his only way out is forming cohesiveness with his greatest supporter, his wife.

By acceptance of his real condition, he equips himself with the ability to learn the skills to deal with his problem, and in doing so, he is able to learn how to deal with it. And he sets on a journey to quiet the voices in his head. Of course they do everything possible to keep him trapped within his own mind, but with practice, he learns to ignore them and little by little they begin to lose volume.

His change comes to life in the film's final scene…as fate would have it, John finds himself back at the very place where his insanity first took shape: his college campus. There he is also faced with the visual manifestation of the characters that had long conquered his mind. But as he walks across the façade of the campus, the characters that used to speak to him so boldly are all standing and watching him pass, and for the first time in his life, they are all quiet.

That is the goal in learning how not to cheat; to quiet the old voices we hear that urge us to be cheaters.

A man's natural inner voice may never change from wanting to be with multiple women, and there is nothing wrong with that. We shouldn't feel guilty for being men. Our inner bad boy may always want to live as it did in the jungles, roaming free without consequence. But we can learn to quiet that voice forever, as John Forbes Nash did in *A Beautiful Mind*.

Cheaters function without rationalizing their actions or the consequences of them. Their internal voice of reason hasn't been strengthened and thusly, they don't have touch with reason.

Learning to control our inner voice so that it doesn't control us ensures that we make better decisions.

We all know that inner-change starts with self-realization. Without it, we continue to live in a false reality and believe that our actions are normal and sane. This is exactly how cheating became normalized within the global male community; there was no attention paid to providing young males with an education on the needed fundamentals to have healthy relationships.

But as I said earlier, "A sane man knows he is insane." And in that truthful self-realization that we are cheaters, we can learn to recondition our inner voices to function as they should—quietly.

The Different
Types of Cheaters

Very often it's necessary to put a title on an issue in order to be able to identify it clearly; somehow cheating has managed to slide by us without adopting any popular terms.

I've taken the liberty to create identities for the various types of cheating men that are out there. So don't be surprised if you find that you are one of them or that you know or are involved with one.

THE "CORPORATE" CHEATER

This is the guy who utilizes his job as his cheating grounds. He finds women that are accessible on his job and business trips. He is normally found to have affairs with his assistant, secretary, or his female business affiliates and uses corporate trips as his cheating portal. A very efficient man, he may often have his side woman help disguise his movements.

THE "IT WASN'T ME" CHEATER

One of the most common cheaters...this cheater is foolishly obvious with his infidelities as he usually learns his cheating skills socially from discussing his exploits with other novice cheaters. When caught with another woman, which shouldn't be at all surprising, he will always extol that the guy a woman believes she's caught wasn't him.

THE "CAREER" CHEATER

This man has cheated for as long as he can remember and cheating on a woman is his full-time occupation. He has made a career of it and treats it like a business...keeping schedules and appointments so tight that they run like clockwork.

THE "LIFER" CHEATER

Older and experienced, the Lifer has been around the block in age and women. He is stuck in a time warp and still needs to feel that he's got the skills to get a variety of women. His mature age allows him the arrogance to believe that he knows and understands all women, but he has never been honest enough with himself to see that he's his own worst enemy.

THE "WEEKEND" CHEATER

This guy is an opportunist...he likes to party and when he gets an opportunity to do so, he takes full advantage of it. Often loud and outrageous, he likes to hit the fast spots (such as Vegas and Miami) for a weekend with his boys and knows the spots where he can have a quick fling without the high risk of getting caught back home.

THE "LOOKING FOR WIFEY" CHEATER

This is a man who truly believes that he is searching for the perfect wife for himself...this is what makes him dangerous. He will cheat in the name of what he believes is his true search for a better woman for himself and cast a line to any woman that he feels could take the current woman's spot. The problem is that he doesn't end one relationship before he starts another.

THE "DIRT-BAG" CHEATER

He is the kind of guy that takes his cheating home. He has virtually no shame in where he does it, as long as he gets to do it. This guy will have sex with another woman in the same bed that he sleeps with his wife in. He is sloppy, so he may not use protection and is known to spread diseases and even get women pregnant that he's cheated with. He is a true dirt-bag because everyone knows that, even for cheaters, there are some things you simply don't do.

THE "SOCIAL NETWORK" CHEATER (AKA THE SNC)

The craftiest and possibly the most savvy of them all…the Social Network cheater uses Facebook, MySpace, BlackPlanet, Hi5, Twitter and other social networks to find women. He maintains a secret profile and may not post his personal photo. He keeps his accounts and passwords hidden and may use a headless picture of his body or a group shot whereby he can tell interested women which face is his, once he solicits them.

No Color Lines

Is cheating color biased? Some women tend to fool themselves into believing that men cheat based on their nationality or faith. More particularly, they also believe that certain ethnic groups are more prone to cheating than others.

So, as not to be biased, I polled ten men of various ethnic descents and nationalities to see who cheated. Three of them were African American from my neighborhood; two were Caucasian, of which one was American and one Australian; the other five were Filipino, Jamaican, West Indian, Korean and one was biracial and homosexual. I point this out because I believe it makes the obvious statement that heterosexual men and gay men are not that different when it comes to cheating.

Out of all ten men, nine admitted they had cheated, including the male that was gay…that's 90 percent!

I then polled ten females to see why they felt 90 percent of these men had cheated. I wasn't surprised to hear the various answers. The commonality in all of them was the belief that men cheat because women let them get away with it. I disagreed and citing my poll, I pointed out that the homosexual male cheated just the same as the heterosexual men and that the determining factor of doing so didn't change much between the two groups, if at all.

Clearly, cheating does not have a color line when it comes to men. However, certain ethnicities are demonized more than others. I have to say that I do see men of color getting the cheating finger pointed at them in pop culture more than other ethnic groups. However, to my experience, other ethnicities cheat just as much if not more; they simply do it with a different swagger.

For instance, because of our innate need to be the biggest lion in the jungle, African-American men may brag about cheating more openly. Men of other groups may therefore seem to have a less ostentatious approach to it, which gives the appearance that they don't cheat as much. But in a circle of men—black, brown, yellow, red and white—they all cheat the same.

Are Tiger Woods, Oscar De La Hoya and Arnold Schwarzenegger the same color? No! So don't believe the hype about color playing a factor in cheating. The fact that all of these men have cheated demonstrates that race is indeed not a factor at all. No matter how much people ignore it, the problem with male cheating is not the bias of our color, it is that none of us have ever been taught how not to cheat.

The New Cheating—
Social Network Cheating

Imagine you're back in 1995 and your name is Larry Brilliant. You have an idea for an Internet platform that will build a playground in cyberspace for people to network with each other.

What you think is a good idea turns out to be the formation of a new social medium that will revolutionize the world of networking, so you call it Social Networking.

Within a decade after you introduce your idea, it skyrockets and spawns other companies that take over the space. Within no time, new companies are born that exceed your highest expectations; they are called Facebook and Twitter.

In your own brilliance, you always knew that your idea would be huge if it caught on. But what you never imagined is in its revolutionary abilities, your concept for a better way to communicate across the Internet would be the breeding ground for the most concentrated cases of cheating that relationships have ever seen. And during those late nights at your computer where you thought you were writing codes and concepts, you actually invented the platform for what we now know as "Social Network Cheating," also known as SNC.

When I talk about this SNC with people, they usually ask me to explain exactly what it is. Social Network Cheating (SNC) is when someone uses a social network site to cheat on his or her mate.

"Cheating online...how do people do that?" they ask me.

This new form of cheating has become one of the most deceptive and dangerous ways to hide infidelity because it easily goes undetected by any unassuming mate with very little effort. It doesn't take much to make a fake name and open a Facebook or Twitter account in this day and age, and once you've made your password private, you're almost impossible to catch unless someone finds you in the act.

For anyone thinking about cheating, SNC makes it easy because there is very little risk and no money needed. That makes it more enticing for cheating men who normally have to invent unique ways to sneak around. SNC means they no longer have to physically hide out or mock up phony cell phone bills to maintain discreet relationships. All they need is a computer and a social networking account and the Internet supplies the rest.

It's gotten so popular that online sites dedicated to cheating are beginning to sprout up quickly to meet the growing demand of people that want to try their hand at low-risk cheating. Even adult entertainment companies are casting their nets for a piece of the traffic that Facebook has cornered in hopes that people with cheating in mind will join their sites.

The emergence of SNC has forced us all to finally ask the question, exactly what is cheating today? Is a man actually cheating if he only has secret non-physical indiscretions online?

To illustrate how far SNC has re-spun the question of cheating, look at the charges placed against Congressman Anthony Weiner. In 2011 the congressman joined the ranks of public officials that were charged with cheating on their wives. But his case of cheating was unlike any other public official before him because he allegedly never had sex or physical contact with anyone.

In actuality, Congressman Weiner didn't really do anything that would be considered cheating by traditional standards. You see, cheating used to be defined by someone having a sexual or physical act outside of their marriage or committed relationship.

But Congressman Weiner participated in the New Cheating—by having secret, sexually explicit exchanges with women on Facebook that his wife didn't know about. After he got away with that, his desires grew and the

Facebook conversations weren't enough. So, as it is with most participants in SNC, he graduated to sending women suggestive photos of himself on Twitter; showcasing that he'd lost touch with consequences and had become a cyber slut.

WHAT IS A CYBER SLUT?

This is what I call men and women that form an addiction to SNC. They can't control themselves and go to extremes to fulfill their SNC lusts. There are no rules because in their minds they aren't technically cheating by traditional standards as there is no physical sex involved.

So they have been free to sneak around without any conviction. Or maybe, like Weiner, they don't understand the gravity of the Internet.

WHERE DO WE GO FROM HERE?

Access by any means necessary! That's the new motto for today's cheater.

They have it and demand it faster and faster every day.

I remember that only a few years ago, a stolen or leaked sex tape was the crazy thing in the media. Now those are seen as frail attempts to rebuild celebrity careers and social networking has become the forbidden fruit.

And with more people using social networking sites to cheat, more divorce lawyers are returning to the scene of the crime for evidence, the *New York Post* reported in 2011.

U.S. divorce courts have become inundated with the social network files of cheaters. A recent poll shows 81 percent of matrimonial lawyers saying that in the past five years, there has been a huge spike in the use of social-networking information as evidence of infidelity.

It even has its own name—"Cyber Evidence."

The most often used cyber evidence includes Facebook messages to secret lovers and incriminating photos found on Twitter, such as in Congressman Weiner's case, a survey from the American Academy of Matrimonial Lawyers reveals.

Make no mistake, that isn't slowing it down. All stats show that the amount of SNC reported is increasing and there are new sites popping up daily to make sure of it.

SNC is the truest indication that the more our world grows, the more opportunities we will have to cheat. So what can the average person do to protect against it?

Believe it or not, there are actually online private detectives for the job, along with various devices that can monitor your mate's computer dialogue on their Twitter and Facebook accounts. And if you really want to go there, you can secretly monitor all of the typed activity on someone's computer. The technology is out there.

But believe me, once you get started you'll be digging down that rabbit hole forever until you find what you're looking for—if you ever find it.

The only true way to protect against a mate that cheats on line is by creating New Monogamy where your mate can be transparent about his/her desires; and more specifically, by equipping males with the capability to be faithful and committed. That is the only way to combat the ever-growing epidemic of cheating as we continue the conversation about learning how not to cheat in this modernized world.

Lies Cheaters Tell

Cheaters come in all shapes, sizes and colors, and their lies are as diverse as they are. It's harder to decipher if you're being cheated on today because the cheating culture has grown so much and with it, so have the lies cheaters tell. Here are a few of the typical lies that cheaters use.

Remember, just because you may have heard one of these lies doesn't mean your mate is cheating.

IT WASN'T ME

This lie is used so much that it became famous as a hit song by Shaggy in the '90s…it teaches cheaters that no matter what a woman says, they should lie to the end.

If her friends catch you with a girl in the club; if her sister says she saw you crossing the street arm in arm; even if they are caught in bed with someone else—no matter what a cheater is told, they will simply declare, "It wasn't me."

JUST A FRIEND

When a couple is committed, any friends from their single lives must become friends of the relationship. But a cheater likes to make his or her exploits seem as if they are only friends. So if your mate is keeping a friend of the opposite sex away from the relationship, then there is a good chance they are or were more than a friend.

YOUR FRIENDS ARE JEALOUS

This is one that cheaters like to use whenever their mates' friends accuse them of cheating. It's easy to use because there is always the chance that the friends are actually jealous. But if you have real friends, then you know their intentions, and a real friend would never try to tear apart a relationship because of jealousy. So if they are really a true friend, then you should heed their words.

I DON'T EVEN KNOW HER

This one is for the male cheaters...we like to use it when a strange female pops up on our cell phone or our mate finds traces of a new woman linked to us. Look at it like this: if her name, email or photo are in his phone, he knows her.

CALLING FROM THE BATHROOM

Cheaters like to call from bathrooms because it disguises the noise from the room or the person they are actually around. If they are in a place they shouldn't be or with someone that they shouldn't be with, then the bathroom is the perfect sound barrier to shield suspicion.

IT'S LADIES NIGHT / WEEKEND

This one is for the ladies...there is absolutely nothing wrong with a ladies night or weekend out. The spa, yoga retreat or spiritual empowerment seminar are all very good reasons for women to do their thing. But if a woman is having ladies night every night or weekly sabbaticals, then it may be a different type of ladies night she's looking for.

KEEPING IT REAL

How far can we go before enough is enough? How far do we believe that we can push someone before they snap and lose their ability to trust us, or anyone else ever again? That is exactly what happens when we keep lying and denying the truth about our cheating. The lies pile up and we end up ruining another person's life. Not because we don't care for or even love them, but because we haven't learned to be truthful with ourselves.

Eventually the lies will come out and the person that's been deceived goes away damaged and is very rarely, if ever, able to trust again.

This is not to imply that there is no life after a cheater; I've personally been able to move ahead to a healthy life after being cheated on. But sometimes it's not easy once you've been deceived and some people never fully recover. That means that the next person they meet has to deal with the last person's lies. Is that fair? No, it isn't!

So before you accept any old excuse, it's okay to demand that your mate is transparent with you, and examine things closely if you feel they aren't. Trust is earned and if they are honest, they will have no problem showing you who they are. Once they've done that, then acceptance and trust should follow. However, if they're being deceitful like the things we covered here and you still fall for it...the joke is on you.

Five Myths Why Men Cheat

Lots of people base their belief of what will cause a man to cheat on hearsay. There are so many myths that misguide us every day into forming prejudices and keep us from learning the true signs that someone will cheat or is cheating.

Both men and women equally share in these beliefs and spread them without even realizing it. In order to really find out the truth about why men cheat, we will have to forego passing these myths and others like them around and accept the truth.

The following are some of the more popular myths that men have said are the reasons they cheat:

God made man in his image (not women).

Man was put on earth to procreate.

Women were put on the earth to be man's companion.

Women are the lesser creature (to man).

Women were made from the rib of a man.

Five Myths Women Consider Cheating

There is a fine line between myth and truth. "In the absence of truth, print the myth" is a very old belief. For many women, that is how the various myths and legends that play on their insecurities are formed.

Over centuries women have spread various myths amongst themselves that shaped the mindsets of the modern woman's viewpoint on what cheating is.

Of all of the myths listed here, I find the one about the player to be the most intriguing. Let's take a closer look at how this myth has shaped the minds of generations of women to overlook the truth that Mr. Right might just be found in Mr. Right Now.

The following are but a few of those unsubstantiated myths that have become the most popular:

Checking out someone of the opposite sex

Fantasizing about another woman

Watching adult movies behind a woman's back

Staying in contact with an ex

Being a player (even when a man is honest)

The Difference Between A Cheater and A Player

Player (Playa): A dramatic actor; One who plays any game;
A gamester; A gambler; One who plays, or amuses himself;
One without serious aims; An idler; A trifler.

The term "player" (aka "playa") has become one of the most misinterpreted, misunderstood and misused terms in popular, social and urban culture to date. The true meaning of the word "player" is "A man who is transparent and honest about having multiple female companions, who agree to share him openly." Such a man seemingly only exists alongside the myths of the Easter Bunny and Bigfoot, because you've probably seen as many of them as you have a real player.

Other slang terms like "pimp" and "hustler" became popular during the 1970s boom of street life, a period that gave men with a slick gift of gab the ability to utilize their negotiating skills to manage the lives of working girls (prostitutes).

Fast-forward to today's pop culture and we find that rappers and reality shows now associate pimps and hustlers with the player, but by definition they have absolutely nothing to do with the player. And it is this mistake that has given the player a bad name, for nothing is truly wrong or flawed with being a player.

A real player is not a cheater…he is honest and up front and while many people won't admit it, he is blatantly disciplined. Refusing to lie and belittle himself for the sake of seducing any woman is his Modus Operandi. That's why when a woman gets disappointed that she can't have him all to herself, a player may very confidently tell her, "Don't hate the player; hate the game."

Why then are women so afraid of the player?

Strongly because women are preconditioned to believe that all men are natural-born liars and that any man that doesn't appear to lie, is doing exactly that. This is hard to accept when women are all too often crushed by the lies of cheating men...so to debunk the player for being honest would be a contradiction, wouldn't it?

Unfortunately, that is exactly the problem between women and players. Women are afraid of truthful men, which makes the truthful player seem like a liar and a contradiction; and as his aberrational ways are so often mis-understood, so is his intent.

The player has truly received a bad rap. Over centuries mainstream society has frowned on him, never acknowledging that his pursuits are the closest thing to a polyamorous man.

How is that, you might ask? Let's examine him more closely and see what attributes the player truly presents for women.

It is widely believed that man is a naturally polyamorous creature who, in his most natural state, desires to be free to have multiple relationships with women. However, through centuries of demand, he has been conditioned to believe that polyamory is not right nor is it acceptable. Even when he's been open and honest about himself, he has been told that his desire to have open relationships is detrimental to women and the family unit.

But in a strange twist, the player may be the perfect man for today's modern women, simply because he is currently the only man that can most certainly be expected to be honest. He will not cheat and although he is emotionally unavailable, his ethics may be perfect for modern women who, because of man's lifestyle of cheating, have focused their energies on career pursuits over finding a husband. The careers of modern women have taken them out of position to engage in the daily disciplines of a monogamous relationship and prevented them from being able to focus on the more traditional confines of a committed relationship.

For this type of modern woman, the player presents an alternative to cheating men. His goal is to have multiple women with no hassle so he is forthcoming and transparent and does not hesitate to remind a woman that he is not interested in being monogamous. And while his pursuits may keep him from spending time with the same woman on a regular basis, he must be disciplined enough to make himself available to the various women that he is dating.

The player's added value is that his strong sense of self-esteem also aides in his ability to maintain principles of safe sex...some women may see him as a risk, but a true player doesn't play himself.

Lastly and most importantly, a true player isn't out to break a woman's heart. He puts his exact interests in a woman on front street, ensuring that she knows at all times where she stands with him, even when she may not like it. He is not afraid to lose her (which is why most men lie) and she will never be able to say that he didn't tell her the truth.

Women can also look at the player as a friend. In fact, the player thinks of the women he is dating as friends, so he won't allow himself to trick them into wanting a monogamous relationship with him. Instead, he keeps things light so women understand that the relationship is not serious.

A real player also encourages women to get their own thing. He isn't demeaning or abusive to keep a woman down like the pimps or hustlers seen on television. Instead, he makes sure he educates a woman on the game of men and gives the modern woman her space to pursue her dreams, goals and aspirations. And while he may be a temporary fix for the woman that is interested in a more monogamous relationship, he may present her with a needed breath of fresh air while the rest of the male species gets its act together and learns how not to cheat.

Great Men Do Cheat

History is a powerful thing. Using it to interpret past events transformed into our modern language to resemble something that is objectively unbiased is impossible to do; and as I have a specific agenda here, I will do my best with the following examples to shed light without trampling on the true historical value or the greatness of the achievements of these great individuals. —MAXWELL BILLIEON

Many people think that being of greatness means you have no flaws. This is why people are always shocked to hear that their favorite politician, social icon or religious leader has cheated or fallen to infidelity.

The truth is, many of the greatest men in our modern and historical societies have cheated and even fathered children outside of monogamous relationships—indeed, they were cheaters. Why is it that men of such personal character, dignity and moral cause could not control their desires to have intimate relationships outside of the confines of a committed relationship?

I literally could have written a book on them alone, as they include a vast array of kings, princes, emperors, diplomats, celebrities and presidents. Look at John F. Kennedy. Considered to have been, or potentially would have become, the greatest American president in the history of the USA. President Kennedy studied at Harvard, stood for the rights of humankind and was honored for servicing his country through World War II.

JFK, as many called him, was the youngest president to have ever been elected at the age of forty-three and the only president to ever win a Pulitzer Prize, an accomplishment not many people will ever achieve.

JFK met his wife, Jacqueline Bouvier, who many consider the first "First Lady" of our nation, because of her elegance, grace and charm, just before he had to face an ongoing battle with Addison's disease, that challenged him very early in their relationship. But Jackie stood by him, nurturing him through four spinal surgeries and what his doctors said was surely his death.

Watching him receive a priest's last rites on his deathbed, Jackie never faltered or wavered from JFK's side. Her intense love and support for him was later to be immortalized for the world to see, when Jackie was filmed reaching over the trunk of the car carrying her husband down Pennsylvania Avenue to retrieve a piece of JFK's head, after he'd been shot.

Truly, in all of Kennedy's accomplishments, his greatest ever was marrying Jackie.

However, having a woman who to her own credit was very attractive and of a high social class, did not keep JFK from exploits with other women... most notably, Marilyn Monroe.

Yes, the president who implemented the Presidential Commission on the Status of Women was said to have had a long affair with the platinum bombshell.

But even before Marilyn, Kennedy was charged with having other affairs that included a sexual romp with Pamela Turnure during his post as a U.S. senator. In a strange twist of life, Turnure later became Jackie's personal secretary in the White House.

And cheating even ensnared our beloved Dr. Martin Luther King Jr. Dr. King's accolades, needless to say, precede any description I could give here. As the face of the Civil Rights Movement and America's fight against racism, Dr. King represented America's move toward equality.

A man of true substance and dignity, Dr. King was esteemed by those of the highest moral and social achievements, including Gandhi, John Lennon, Robert and John Kennedy, and to his credit, he was revered by people who chose to stand against the moral, spiritual and inalienable rights of all human beings of color.

With all that he stood for and had achieved, he still admittedly cheated on his loving and faithful wife, Coretta Scott King. It is said that Dr. King told his wife of not one mistress, but several. For many people, this is impossible to believe about the more than deserving winner of the Nobel Peace Prize.

Needless to say, there have been many other men in world history who have achieved great standing, but have also fallen to the strong hold of cheating. Some of the more influential names include Napoleon, Thomas Jefferson and Bill Clinton…he, as we all remember, had a very public and harsh reckoning with infidelity in what almost resulted in his impeachment from office.

Why do the marital infidelities of these great men leave scars on their achievements? Is it fair that their legacies are stained due to monogamous betrayal?

Who is perfect enough to suggest that any human, male or female, should ultimately be defined by their indiscretions? Even though, as Dr. King stated, "A man should be judged by the content of his character," men are all too often characterized by their lack of character displayed when it comes to monogamy. And if such judgment of man is correct, then even the great Dr. King would be considered a failure.

Maybe it's time that America stopped expecting prominent men to be more than human. I'm not making excuses for these men because what they all did bears severe consequence, not only for them but also for their wives. But I believe that they are also victims of cheating. America and even the world puts far too much emphasis on perfection and that is impossible to achieve.

We continue to expect men of power to be inhumanly perfect, and when they show us that they are in fact just like us, we crucify them. Without a doubt, great men have more of a responsibility to be morally upright, but the burden of traditional monogamy has proved to be too heavy for even the strongest of shoulders.

Again, I do admit that there should be a penalty for their cheating, but it should include forgiveness and rehabilitation. It doesn't make sense that we expect men to be great at monogamy unless we rehabilitate their minds. The rehabilitation I am speaking of comes by educating males on the principles of monogamy and polyamory, along with the acceptance of women of what men truly are.

It's time to wake up, America, and accept the truth. We know how to train males to achieve greatness. So if we take steps to educate males on how to achieve greatness in relationships, we can then, and only then, expect that they will be able to achieve true greatness in monogamy.

Battle of the Sexes

Ten-thirty a.m.—Los Angeles time on Friday, the Fourth of July holiday weekend. I was in my office when I got a phone call from my friend Christine. She is a highly intelligent and educated professional African-American woman that believes she's never been cheated on. Consequently, she has no problem expressing her opinions about the issues of male cheating.

She always loves to remind me of this fact by stating, "Men don't cheat on me because they know that I won't tolerate it. If a man ever did, he'd be out faster than he could say I'm sorry."

We've had many conversations about why men cheat, but this particular phone call was not about why; it was more of a note to all men on the issue of cheating, which she felt was important to point out to me first, because I am the arbiter of the cheating male species.

As soon as I got on the phone, I could tell she was turned up about something. The excitement in her voice was about Tiger Woods' divorce settlement. Christine had heard a rumor that his wife was potentially getting $750 million in the divorce settlement. To her, that news was the shot from the heavens to all men that cheating would now truly cost us everything. And she wasn't merely happy; she was so exhilarated by the news that she told me that she and her friends were thinking of starting an Internet fan page for Tiger's ex. I asked her, "What would make you guys do something like that?" She responded, "His wife is our *shero*!"

It became immediately obvious to me that this was clearly a case where, along with Christine, the female community felt some solidarity with Tiger's wife. For them, the statement was much bigger than Tiger. The heavy penalty put on him was a testament in the battle of the sexes that women had scored a fatal blow against cheating men.

I nudged her a bit, stating that Tiger was rich before he met his wife and that the story was probably false news from a tabloid anyway.

"I don't care; he's getting his just due and now men will see that women aren't going to sit by and be played any longer," she emphatically stated.

I was a little bit surprised at Christine's vigor because traditionally, African-American women don't side with a woman like Tiger's wife. First of all, many of them still have issues with African-American men marrying women of other ethnicities.

However, in Tiger's case, women were putting a flag down and stating that they no longer feel they need to abide by the traditional or cheating ways of men in relationships. They were gonna use TW to make a painful example for all men to see that getting cheated on is no longer an option. That is a bold stance when compared to any generation before them.

I have noticed that when many of my male and female friends and colleagues discuss the issue of cheating, they do it as though it's "us vs. them." There is indeed a battle between men and women raging over cheating—a veritable "battle of the sexes." For centuries men have played the cheating game with no expectation of consequence and it has instilled fear in women. As is the case in any battle, the person living in fear eventually decides to fight back and this time they are women.

I was in what should have been a very serious relationship for years before I'd learned how not to cheat. Once I'd learned how not to cheat, I gained a serious desire to have a more committed relationship.

One day I told her that I wanted to get married and work on building a family; however, to my surprise she wouldn't commit to it. She stated to me that she wasn't afraid of not getting married or having a child anymore.

Hunh?

That statement shocked me and served to wake me up to the realization that because of her suspicions that I was cheating, although I was never caught, she'd become so afraid that she'd given up hope that we'd ever have a future or family together. And although she didn't have the strength to break up with me, she wasn't going to take a chance on building a life with me, either.

That is the new attitude of the female community at large. They no longer want to continue building their lives with cheating men, nor should they. So as much as I hated to, I had to agree with Christine that Tiger's cheating brought about his own downward spiral leading to the ineluctable breakup of his family. Nor could I disagree that his wife deserved some compensation for her pain and suffering, although Tiger is the one that crashed into a tree.

However, I had to remind her that Tiger is also a victim, believe it or not.

Of course, her response was, "Maxwell, you are crazy; how can you possibly say such a thing?" But if women can briefly put aside the anger they feel because of Tiger's cheating to examine how and why it happened, they will see that Tiger is also the victim.

I say Tiger is a victim because he was bred to be a cheater without his consent. No one ever taught him how not to cheat, but they expected him to be faithful—we all did. None of us would like it if we were expected to deliver something that we weren't taught to deliver.

This is not an excuse, but it is the reason that he cheated. He still has to pay the consequences of his actions, but we should back up for a minute to learn from his life and not simply point our fingers of humiliation. Better that we come to terms with what Tiger truly is, or we may wake up and find that Tiger's problem has become our own.

Tiger Woods:
The Cheating Prophet

Many years ago, stories about the achievements of men were used as examples of what should be done to be better, moral and respected. As prophets, these morally upstanding men were believed to have been closer to God and carried great teachings of wisdom from place to place.

Humankind has continued to hold such men high above normal stature, as the model that we should all aspire to be.

But the modern era has changed all that and today we are more inclined to learn from the mistakes of men, than from their achievements. As long as we learn, I don't see anything wrong with that. What is a prophet anyway but someone whose life is an example for others to learn from?

My rationalization for referring to Tiger Woods as a prophet is based on the evidence that he has been placed in our lives to be an example of the detriment that men face if they continue to cheat. Look at Tiger's life and you'll see that the writing is on the wall that if we do not heed Tiger's mistakes, then we are next to fall.

So many men reading this may be thinking that they aren't sloppy like Tiger or that they can never get caught. Yes, Tiger was sloppy and it is easy to feel contempt for his lack of skills. But men, if our goal is to continue the pursuit of cheating because we don't think we'll ever get caught, then we are doomed. You *will* get caught and it will affect you, your mate and your family, just like Tiger.

But Tiger's life went wrong well before he ever cheated. Like so many other men, he was guided down the path of self-destruction way before he was married. Then, once his options became vast, he didn't have the skills to detect the consequences of his actions. It was too late for him, as he could not have recognized the signs of his slow death without someone wiser than him providing him with an education.

Where were those men of higher relationship intellect and experience for Tiger?

Their absence is not his fault, but learning the lessons became his responsibility. While we'd love to think that someone had to have said something to Tiger about his cheating at some point in time, where was the guru who could have given him the tools to aid him in guarding against his mind and body, as they betrayed his better judgment?

Let us learn from the failure of the men who neglected to teach Tiger when he was a cub how to function in a society that now requires men to know the art of monogamy, or the truth of being polyamorous.

As with all men, Tiger's cheating issues start at an adolescent level. Although he did not mean to, his father, by not teaching Tiger how *not* to cheat, taught him *to* cheat.

Men work the opposite of females, who do not need a mother to teach them how to be faithful, feminine and nurturing. Females are simply born with it and their mothers help cultivate it as they grow. As they mature, they take their natural instinct to nurture a man into a committed relationship.

On the flip-side of that are men. We aren't nurturing so we require male mentors to teach us how to cultivate a relationship. If we don't have these mentors, then we follow our instincts and they are the opposite of women's. Women nurture and men conquer!

You can be assured that if Tiger would've had a cheating mentor, then he would be just as great at monogamy, or polyamory, as he is at golf. Learning how not to cheat is a lot like the game of golf; in order to master it, you have to practice and learn from the best.

No one taught Tiger's father, so Tiger's father didn't teach him. So the next time you see Tiger in his Sunday red, swinging full speed off the tee box, picture him in a long, flowing white linen robe, with his golf clubs as tablets of commandments or scrolls of information. Maybe that will help you see the real prophet that Tiger is and learn from his mistakes instead of going through life and relationships screaming, "Fore!"

Why Do Powerful Men Cheat So Badly?

Women searched for an answer to this question long before any of us existed on this planet. With more and more men being caught cheating, the answer is finally becoming increasingly clear—it's simply because they can!

Or should I say because women and government enable them to? The last time I checked, cheating on a woman wasn't illegal in any state in America. You can't go to jail for cheating on your wife, but you can if you cheat on your taxes. So which one should be more important to a powerful man?

But that's a small part of the issue, because whether you believe it or not, powerful men don't cheat worse than regular men; men in general cheat badly. We don't have to be rich, famous or powerful to cheat without conscience. Let me give you a couple of examples of this bad cheating from men that I've experienced personally.

If you think Schwarzenegger is bad, I once knew a city bus driver who fathered twelve children by twelve different women. He was also married during half of the affairs. The kicker is that some of them knew about the others and some did not. At least Arnold took care of his secret child. This guy didn't take care of any of them. He lived on a bus driver's salary, and with all due deference to bus drivers, twelve children is out of the budget.

But wait, it gets worse. I also know a guy whose great-grandfather moved from his Asian homeland to America and fathered thirteen children by thirteen women. He also had three other children by his wife back home—the woman he somehow conveniently forgot to divorce before he left for the States. Virile old grandpa wasn't rich, either; he was a regular blue-collar, working guy. Now that gives an entirely different meaning to the term "working man's stiff."

Neither of these men, or the countless men like them around the world, had power like Bill Clinton or John Edwards; and they weren't celebrities like Tiger Woods, Charlie Sheen or Oscar De La Hoya, all of whom cheated on their wives. However, these men cheated just as badly, and the trappings of power aren't an excuse as to why they did what they did.

Regular guys don't have trains, planes and automobiles at their disposal to help fulfill their every lust or desire. So if a man can cheat with twelve different women on a bus driver's pay, then what's to curb his enthusiasm when he's rich or famous?

If you really think about it, the power ultimately lies with the women, not the men. Powerful men can cheat so badly because weaker women enable them to cheat. Not that all women who become a man's mistress are aware that the man is using them to cheat, but if we look at the recent cases of celebrity and political cheating all of the women involved in the cheating scandals were 100 percent aware that the men were married. And they got down with it anyway.

So who is really to blame?

Should Sandra Bullock only blame Jesse, or also the women he was sleeping with?

The real question is why don't some women care that they are being used? Perhaps it's because America has created a "get it while you can" mentality and if you don't, then you are somehow weak or stupid.

You may remember that only one of the women that Tiger cheated with said that he'd promised to be with her. The other women didn't care and didn't think twice about his wife or what his cheating would do to his family. They looked out for themselves, and not very well, I might add. You tell me; if you are gonna cheat with a man worth that much, don't you think you should get more than a free trip or sex in the back of a truck? I'm not a woman but as a former cheater, game recognizes game.

The question of why the power of men like Tiger equates to sexual privilege is very sensitive. Do fame and power make sex more readily available—absolutely! Because there are always women who will only look out for what they can get temporarily and that enables a man to cheat.

Many social biologists argue that these women weaken a man's ability to have self-restraint. But I say that a man's lack of development is the reason he has no self-restraint. That's why Ray J wasn't able to resist having spontaneous sex with a strange woman in a gas station bathroom while his girlfriend waited for him at home...but we'll get to that later. The bottom line is that he was never taught to internalize any barriers or rules to govern his thinking in relationships. That's also why most men have an "anything goes" attitude and don't see that their actions are harmful.

Why else would Schwarzenegger be able to sleep with the housekeeper behind his wife's back? There was no internal alarm to go off and tell him, "Wait, this is over the edge." Many powerful, famous and rich men cannot internally forecast the results of their cheating because they do not have what I like to call the "Consequence Mechanism." Without this consequence mechanism, men can't see the consequences, or should I say that men don't have the internal voice to warn them of the consequences of their actions when it comes to cheating.

Women want to believe that certain things, like not getting your house-keeper pregnant behind your wife's back, should be common sense. But common sense is based on having an ability to foresee consequences, and most men aren't bred with that ability when it comes to monogamous relationships.

It may sound like a cop-out but look at it from this perspective.

Society doesn't breed young boys into "Thinking Men" that rationalize consequences based on what is healthy behavior in committed relationships. We direct their attention to seeing life as a series of cases of right vs. wrong, but the problem is that they can't use the right vs. wrong principle in relationships because men don't believe that monogamy is right.

That's why I say right and wrong are dead—long live consequence!

Women are bred with the consequence mechanism and up until this century, a woman's ability to get a powerful man was based on the consequences of her actions. If she achieved things such as looks, education, or social status, then the odds were higher that she'd get a "good" man. But it's the opposite for guys; we have been able to get women simply because we are men, and that has caused us to have God Complex. We don't need a degree or riches to get a "good" woman, so once a man achieves power, he naturally feels he can just about have anything.

We will never see a change in this issue until we start breeding young males with the consequence mechanism and re-educating adult males on the principles of consequence. That is the only way to achieve a shift in the arrogance that we men have when dealing with power.

What is power anyway? Traditionally, power means having a high position. And it can also be perceived as having money or fame. But true power comes from having power over the minds of people. That is the most deadly power of all—the power of perception.

The power of perception makes people think that you can do things you can't do. It makes a less savvy thinker believe a poor man is rich and a bad man is good; or that a group of people are closer to God than you are.

When you are able to shape perception, you have the power to create an alternate reality for others, and that is more powerful than any position or money you can create.

An example of this is the perception of the president of the United States. The title sounds far more powerful than the actual position. Is the president more powerful than the people?

No.

It was Barack Obama's ability to show this fact to Americans that motivated us to vote for him. His model caused us to believe that we could change things together. The perception of having an African American in what we perceive as the most powerful office in the world, meant change in and of itself...that's the power of perception at work.

So whenever a man who attains that sort of power cheats, it's magnified a thousand times bigger than if your neighborhood dry cleaner did it.

Why?

America has put too much emphasis on the accomplishments of powerful men. They aren't perfect! But America wants to believe that these men have achieved position, money or fame because they are "more perfect" than the normal Joe.

But it's not true…they aren't different and their cheating proves it.

But why do they have to cheat so badly?

The first reason is that a regular guy doesn't have women looking at him as the object of desire. That is too much for most men to handle because it switches the roles of sexual power. Normally, women have that power. Men aren't used to it at all. Only the lucky few 1 percent of men like Obama ever get to achieve that type of desirability.

Powerful men also have less time and more access; that combination is lethal. And let's not forget that these men almost definitely would've cheated whether they were powerful or not, but their power makes weak women easier prey.

What we all need to accept is that monogamy is not an innate skill for men; it's a learned behavior. When women stop enabling men to cheat, men will be forced to refocus their power on the consequences of their actions and that ultimately will lead to creating more faithful men.

Let Them Eat Cake: The Study

Whenever a celebrity gets caught cheating, you can virtually imagine the entire world scream, "Why?" in unison. Almost simultaneously it's posted all around the world via the social spotlight pages of cyberspace.

What the hell is wrong with these guys? Didn't they see the other episodes starring Tiger Woods, John Edwards, Bill Clinton and the other co-stars of powerful debauchery get caught and burned at the stake? Why wasn't all the finger-pointing and shame-on-you coverage enough to prevent them from joining the ranks of popular cheaters?

About 2,000 years ago, Socrates said in Plato's "Phaedrus" that "two horses contend for our souls—one, unruly, passionate and constantly pulling in the direction of pleasure, and the other restrained, dutiful, obedient and governed by a sense of shame." However, I recently read a set of studies conducted by the University of Southern California Marshall School of Business* that suggests that Socrates had it all wrong, at least about Horse No. 2. Humans may be pulled more toward pleasure, but contrary to Socrates' theory, shame isn't the dominant force that pulls us in.

In fact, the more we anticipate having the finger pointed at us in public persecution and guilt, the less we're likely to exhibit self-control. Instead, it seems that when we focus on the exuberance that comes from rising to good behavior, we make much better choices.

USC found out by letting a bunch of people eat cake. In their study, they put three groups of people alone in a room with a big piece of chocolate cake, along with the utensils to eat it. Then they told the groups that they could eat as much cake as they wanted. A little or a lot, it was completely up to them. But before they allowed them to do so, they told the members of group A to focus on the elation they would feel if they resisted eating the high-calorie cake. Then they told the second group to picture the shame they would feel by not resisting it. And finally the last group was allowed to do whatever they wanted without any instructions.

What they found out was that the people that imagined the pride they'd feel from resisting their cravings ate much less than the people that focused more on feeling ashamed for giving in to their cravings. They also ate less than the people with no restrictions. So you see, when it comes to self-restriction, the thought of achieving drives us more than the threat of shame.

But what causes man to respond to anticipated pride better than to threatening shame to resist our temptations? It is seemingly that pride forces us to pay attention to ourselves as well as the success we achieve from it. However, shame focuses on the opposite, placing the attention on the object of our desire and the threat of giving in to it. That makes it so much harder to resist. In other words, the thought of resisting temptation makes us proud and in turn, we feel good about ourselves and that drives us to do it; while anticipating shame makes us feel bad.

Not all bad feelings create the same tendencies when it comes to dealing with self-control. Again, remember that the study also showed that the people that were told to think of the guilt ate more cake. If you think about it, it makes total sense that we would be more motivated to do the right thing by the prospect of feeling good over bad. But can any of this stop men from making poor decisions when faced with having to implement self-control?

You can best believe that throwing handfuls of humiliation or public punishment at powerful men will not curb the next dog from cheating. What we need to do is educate men on how to implement the discipline of foreseeing a positive consequence to ignite the feeling that comes along with resisting temptation.

It's sort of like when you want to resist food to lose weight. Instead of putting a picture of yourself on the wall, you would probably respond best to a photo of the ultimate body you have set as your goal. It's the same for men; staying fixed on the benefits of the commitment helps to see us through the times of temptation.

What USC may not have even realized is that by studying chocolate cake consumption, they may have stumbled on a key element of helping men learn how not to cheat. Such lessons can also be used for anyone facing temptation.

So remember, using shame to try and curb cheating won't work, and guilt may only make it easier to give in to temptation. Instead, try to think about the positive effects of making a good decision. And that's exactly what will happen.

*Study performed by Deborah McInnis, vice dean for research and strategy, and a professor of business administration and marketing at USC.

The Consequences of Cheating

We already know that men are from Mars and women are from Venus and it is vital that we each learn to speak each other's language to have better relationships. But first we must get our basic fundamentals in line as individuals, and the issue of male cheating is at the top of that fundamental list.

Now I don't live in a fairy tale world where I expect everyone to want the same change. After all, no society on planet earth has ever been perfect and no cultural change can be built on monolithic idealism. But I can see that today's women cheat more as the consequence of men's cheating, and that's scary enough for me to see that male cheating has to change.

If you doubt what I'm saying, look at these stats. During recent decades, the female community has modernized at an incredibly fast pace. Only ten years ago 14 percent of women in committed relationships admitted to cheating; today it's 54 percent. Modern women have become hunters in what was once a man's jungle and they have developed better instincts, making them deadlier cheaters than men have ever been.

My realization of this fact was the catalyst to change my own cheating ways because I would rather spend the rest of my life sleeping peacefully with change, than to be haunted by the ill memories of my own cheating past. As the saying goes, "Every dog must learn new tricks."

This millennium should have been a harmonious evolution of the sexes; instead we have millions of women cheating to make the playing field even. And the numbers don't lie.

Until now, man has never had a reason to feel any consequence of his cheating. That's because every ancient doctrine teaches that we men are the preferred sex and that ultimately, we only need women for the purpose of spreading our seed across the planet.

Ancient teachings like this are no longer acceptable by themselves in the modern village...we need a new education. We've finally reached the day and time where right and wrong are no longer relevant...we must all now focus on consequence.

Coming into the new model of letting consequence rule our decisions means that we will act based on the outcome of our actions. Where right and wrong were built on religious precepts, consequence is based on each individual acting responsible for the betterment of the community.

To repair the damage that male cheating has caused women, today's men have to deal with the consequences of our actions by maturing much earlier in life than our fathers did. Early maturity means less mistakes and early advancement.

Simply put, it's time for a new model of thinking about cheating.

The perpetual flow of new models has been the cornerstone of humanities creative and intellectual revolutions throughout history. The great societies of ancient Africa, Rome, Moorish Spain, Egypt, Mayan Civilization, the Harlem Renaissance and many others have flourished on moments in time where men and women have worked together through intellectual thought, invention and re-invention, to spawn new ideas and theories that helped their societies evolve.

Somehow, tackling the issue of male cheating has escaped them all and the consequence has been the downward spiral of male-female relationships on a global scale.

So here I present a new way to think about cheating that begins with a new education and the realization that our age-old teachings are a thing of the past. The new model for relationships is...

Right and wrong are dead—long live consequence!

THE CONSEQUENCES

The evolution of our ideals often pushes us to be optimistic about the future while at the same time, keeping the past in close reference. If we look at man's history of cheating we can see that there has been very little attention paid to its consequences. Truly that has played the prominent role in our failure to evolve. As the saying goes, "Those that forget the past are doomed to repeat it."

Cheating comes with many consequences, none of which are positive, healthy or fruitful. The effects can be damaging beyond repair and may even span generations.

IS IT WORTH IT?

No matter how we perceive

The Consequences of Cheating

Here are a few consequences to help anyone who may need to reflect on what cheating can do:

Permanent loss of trust

Permanent loss of respect

Loss of finances

Unplanned pregnancy and children

Sexual disease

Stalking by an emotionally injured victim

Mental damage

Lawsuit

Divorce

Loss of children

Physical confrontation

Stress

our problems with a mate, the question that should always be asked is, "Is it worth it to cheat?"

For anyone who is or has thought about cheating, considering the consequences before you act may help provide a more informed decision and even provide unexpected introspective. Is there anything positive that can come from infidelity? We must all ask ourselves this sooner or later.

There are many other alternatives to cheating and in consideration of them all, they are all better than cheating. Giving yourself a chance to consider them before you act, may be the saving grace in your relationship as well as your own sanity.

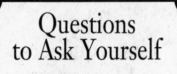

Questions to Ask Yourself

Have I looked for help for my relationship?

Does my mate truly know how I feel?

Should I seek counseling?

Have I considered other alternatives?

What are my options?

Would I be better off leaving?

What is missing in my relationship that is causing me to want to stray?

Is this a pattern in my life?

Am I being impulsive?

Have I been educated on how to stop cheating?

No one is perfect—ergo, no relationship is perfect. Gifting ourselves with all of the tools needed to clear a path through the inner-voices that push us to cheat is our best and most fruitful method to navigating the terrain of relationships in the modern era.

PART II

Conversations With a Cheating Man— The Opening

Sitting in my living room one rainy afternoon in L.A., I prepared to get into a series of discussions about the issues of male cheating with a young celebrity named Ray J. I'm sure you're wondering what would make a celebrity want to talk about the risqué subject of cheating.

Well, one week before that day, he'd expressed to me that he had a problem with cheating on women and wanted to find a way to change, but he didn't know how to. His interest in talking with me was prompted by a conversation we'd had where I told him I was writing a book titled, *Death of the Cheating Man*.

"What's that about?" he asked. I told him that the book was about my own past issues with cheating and how I learned not to cheat.

"C'mon, Maxwell, you ain't telling me that you don't cheat," he chimed in disbelief.

I told him that I had taught myself how to be faithful after many years as a cheater and had held true to it with no problem. He was shocked but not as shocked as he was when I told him that I could do the same for him, if he was willing to be my case study and come clean. "You have to be one hundred percent honest and transparent about everything, or it won't work," I said.

So when he agreed and asked me for help, I gathered that he really wanted to change his cheating ways. But he still seemed pretty skeptical about whether he could actually learn how not to cheat. And I could tell that he really didn't believe that I had beat cheating, either. But his curiosity was enough for me to take the next step and we agreed to get started.

Since my change from cheater, I'd been able to teach my close friends the basic principles of my philosophy of learning how not to cheat. They were all happy with the results, but I wanted to try it out on someone that had an extreme lifestyle like Ray J.

His fame and "anything goes" attitude toward life had taken him in and out of relationships and gotten him into a lot of trouble with women. And frankly speaking, the guy isn't shy about his ability to get multiple women.

Would a guy who had every possible advantage to continue cheating be able to reform? That was the question I wanted to answer for myself.

With him as my case study of the cheating man, my goal was clear: take an in-depth look at why he and men like him, that is to say men with fame or power, cheat—and often cheat so badly and blatantly. If he was honest and diligent in using the principles I would teach him, then I could get him to stop cheating through a process that I call "Making the New Man."

This is the same process that I used to reform my own mind from being a cheating man, into being an honest and transparent-thinking man. And if I did it, then so could any guy who wanted to change. I also told him that in addition to ending his cheating, he would also change other areas of his life and become more responsible for his actions overall.

That's the great thing about learning how not to cheat...you become responsible for your actions all the way around.

To be honest, other than the fact that we both had successful careers in the entertainment industry, I didn't particularly think that Ray and I had much in common. I am a few years older than him, so I wanted to find some common ground between us without making him think that I'd go easy on him because we knew each other.

I kicked things off by telling him about my past issues with cheating, so he could see the level of transparency that I'd expect of him as well.

Surprisingly, he didn't hesitate to jump in with stories about his own life that began to jump out of his head like scenes in a movie. It didn't take long for me to notice that Ray's personal stories sounded all too familiar to me.

He started with the things that most men bragged about behind closed doors. You know, the stuff about how we can get women and the way that we do it, etc., etc., etc. That's sort of how men gossip. It helped get things rolling and from there, we'd be able to flow right into the issue of cheating itself.

Walking through Ray's experiences reminded me of my journey to become a new man and the many things that I'd left behind in my old life as a cheating man.

As we continued the dialogue, we started to throw stories back and forth… it was almost like the way boys play a sword fight game—jousting to see who'd had the crazier life.

I hate to have to say it, but this sort of volleying is common sport for cheating men…guys grow up hearing it all the time and it has become a normal part of the way men congregate. Barbershops, gyms and even golf courses play a regular backdrop to discussions about the females that guys cheat with. It's sort of a twisted male-bonding experience that somehow allows men to achieve camaraderie through debauchery.

Like so many men, Ray's stories of cheating also mimicked scenes from wild movies…cheating in private planes, hotel suites, penthouses, estates, limos, beaches, even a bathroom at a gas station. Just about anything you can imagine had been done to cheat. And over the weeks that followed, I was sure we would cover it all. But in that first conversation, the goal was to get him to answer the real question—the biggest question of them all:

Why do men cheat?

I wanted to hear Ray's perspective of why he felt he and men like him cheated. So to get to the root of it, I asked him to start from the very first time he cheated and I immediately saw that this journey was going to be a crazy ride.

CONVERSATION #1:

The Gift and The Curse: Why Men Cheat

S ince our first conversation, I'd done some thinking about what Ray J had told me regarding the way he'd started cheating. It was time to talk again and I wanted to hear exactly why he thought men like him cheated. That is to say men with fame or power.

You can tell a lot about how a man will apply himself to stop cheating if you know how he looks at cheating naturalistically.

A lot of men believe that we are supposed to cheat—or that we are actually made to be cheaters by nature. Others feel forced into it because of the demands of women and monogamy. The one thing that is universal amongst men is that no matter how much a man wants to stop cheating, if he holds on to those sort of beliefs, then his change will always be short-lived, if it ever comes at all.

The following chapter is a real examination of how men like Ray J often feel about women and why they think they have to cheat on them...until they learn how not to cheat.

RAY J: I feel like every man has to cheat...we are cursed to have to cheat. Just like God cursed women to have periods, men are cursed to cheat because women demand monogamy.

Even scientists agree that it's in the male genetic makeup to need more than one woman. We are animals, like lions and tigers…we hunger to have a pack of women in heat. It's the same in the animal kingdom. There's one dominating male who usually mates with all the females; a whole pride of them and those females are his bitches, to put it in street terms.

It's not a human thing or a black or white thing; it's a male thing.

Back in the day it was all about trying to have a monogamous relationship. But it's not about monogamy anymore. It's more about a man being real with himself and with women, so that he can get back to his true essence of being a man, and that means having multiple women.

If a man could have the woman he loves and he knew for sure that she would never leave or cheat on him…if he really saw the future and knew with certainty that even if he slept with a million women, that his woman would never leave, then he would surely sleep with a million women; that's for sure.

I believe that the main reason why men have not been able to reach this point before is because religion and women have instilled fear in men to believe that our natural state of being is morally wrong. But it's not wrong; we're animals so how could that be wrong?

Look at it like this: After a male lion has sex with all of the lionesses, they don't get an attitude and leave or go cheat on him. Because after he smashes them, there is a natural law that says that those females are his, and no other lion is gonna mess with them. They are living their lives in their natural state of existence.

But human females have way too much information and that has messed up the natural state of things.

Seriously, men shouldn't be trying to learn how to be monogamous; instead we should be trying to get back to our animal state of being like the lions and tigers and simply being our natural selves.

For me, I'm 100 percent down with polyamory.

Why be with one woman? I shouldn't have to cheat because I shouldn't be in the position of having to compromise the animalistic side of my nature. I'm a man and that means that I need to hunt and have sex. That's it!

Women have it so twisted. They think that we are supposed to be like them, but we can't. It's never worked and it never will!

I was always taught that women are nurturers. They aren't meant to hunt like men; they are meant to take what we hunt and prepare it for the family. It's not better or worse; it's just different.

To the modern woman, that sounds chauvinistic; nowadays women are on some independent shit. I personally think that's why more and more of them continue to end up single. They are confused about their roles and think that they should be able to do whatever men can do. So if we cheat, then they should also cheat.

I respect their hustle and that they want to have their own thing to make the playing field even. After all, my mom and sister are independent women who feel that they don't need a man to do anything, so they play more of a man's role in their personal and business lives. That's cool, and if a woman is bringing home the bacon, then she is assuming a man's role.

But we all know that ultimately we will never sit down at a table that is about conquering and have the top dog be a woman. No disrespect, but the odds are against that happening in this crazy world! Women will most definitely be in the room, but the conquering part will always be a man's job. It's the natural order of human society.

If it sounds harsh that I am saying that it's not natural for women to conquer like men, it's only because it's true. It's absolutely unnatural for women to step into that role. If you don't believe me, look at situations where women have to take on that responsibility. It becomes almost impossible for them to do it without taking on the traits of a man. The feminine side of them doesn't like that and they have to pull out the masculine to make it work. Living in a man's role all the time is so unnatural that it's impossible to still be feminine and nurturing at the same time as being masculine.

The problem in the modern era is that women have been removed so far from their natural state of being able to be nurturing that they don't know how to let a man do what we are meant to do. And that's to conquer!

To put it bluntly, men must be able to explore our sexuality without women being jealous or causing drama. It's time that women accept that a man having sex with multiple women has nothing to do with the way we men feel about them—sex for us is no big deal.

Women don't like to hear that, but it's the truth. That's why it's easier for a successful man, especially a celebrity, to have sex with multiple women without wanting a commitment to any of them. Having that option is usually only reserved for beautiful women…most guys never have that option.

That's because when you're a hot woman, everybody wants to get you in bed. But it's not in a woman's genetic makeup to fuck everybody. It causes her to feel like a slut…well, not all women feel that way, but most of them do.

But when a guy has that sort of ability, he wants to fuck all the women, just like the lions and tigers do.

We've all seen guys who get caught up in chasing that lifestyle and never settle down because it's so enticing.

The only thing that keeps most men from having multiple women that way is that they don't have the money to do it. Again, that's why a rich or powerful guy is more prone to get caught cheating. He just doesn't give a fuck; he has too many options and he knows it.

Unfortunately, if you get success, you will probably cheat—it's a gift and a curse.

N eedless to say, I wasn't shocked to hear Ray's limited way of thinking. It wasn't that different from the way that I used to think before I evolved as a man. As Ray sat there running the concept through his mind, I re-engaged the dialogue.

"Ray, it's crazy to think that men can't learn honesty or self-restraint. The truth is that you're wrong; we aren't specifically wired to cheat. The bottom line is that what we really need in order to end our cheating has never been given to us, and that's an education on learning how not to cheat. If not, this cheating epidemic will be the demise of the American family," I said.

"C'mon, Maxwell…you're putting a little too much on it, don't you think? The demise of the human family…that sounds like a movie," Ray joked.

"Think about it. If you woke up tomorrow and found out that women all around the world had been turned into men…that they literally had lost their vaginas and grown penises and their breasts had turned into pecs, that even their behavioral traits had become masculine, what would you do?" I asked.

"Oh hell no! I would scream and literally go crazy!" Ray screamed loud enough to almost break the windows in the room.

"Well, maybe you haven't noticed, but 'women are becoming the new men' to protect themselves from our cheating. In fact 'Women are the new men' and now they cheat just as much as men do. If this continues, it's most definitely the demise of the human family as we know it," I said, hoping he would get it.

"Damn, that's true...women are definitely cheating more now. But it might be too late to stop it. They are pissed at us! That's why I just say screw it and cheat anyway. I feel like I'm cursed to cheat forever," Ray said.

"Now that sounds like a movie," I said jokingly.

"No one is cursed to cheat forever. It's a choice! You have to recognize that, in life, we only know what we're taught, right? Whether we learn by parental or scholastic training or social breeding, we're still being taught what to do and how to behave.

"But when it comes to cheating, we were never taught how to stop it. That's why you haven't stopped and that's why men everywhere still continue to do it, almost against their own wills. There is no curse, just a lack of education. It's time for the re-education of man's miseducation," I said to stamp my point.

"So men cheat because we haven't had an education on how not to cheat," Ray asked himself out loud. "Well, I definitely don't know any man that teaches that class. But I don't think guys would wanna learn that because we aren't gonna admit that cheating is a problem."

"That's true...we don't like to admit that cheating is a problem for us," I said.

"Yea—we feel that admitting there is a problem gives women power over us because they are the ones demanding monogamy," Ray added. "Plus, Maxwell, I seriously can't see myself having just one woman though, and I've never seen any man, rich guy or regular guy, that could be in a relationship without hitting a little something on the side," Ray said, almost accepting defeat.

"You mean you never have until now...I'm one hundred percent monogamous," I said confidently.

"I can't believe it," Ray said in total disbelief.

I could tell that although he still hadn't yet fully accepted that I, or any man, for that matter, could be 100 percent monogamous, he wanted to believe it could happen. But it would take a re-education of his mind to make the difference as we moved ahead to reveal the episodes that shaped his cheating past and the disciplines that would reshape his future with women and relationships.

The Re-Education
of the Male

We males don't realize it but we are born into a community that teaches us self-indulgence and entitlement, simply because we are guys. Most of us are bred with a very limited exposure to discipline, especially in today's world. Society has taken away many of the basic elements that we've needed for relationship evolution in the name of its perceived equal advancement of the sexes.

Consequently, we generally assume that a male will naturally find the necessary maturity he needs for relationships as he comes of age. But with age comes misguided confidence and that confidence when it comes to men comes with a sense of sexual entitlement, it always has. Enter power, money and politics and we go buck-wild because we are missing the fundamental teachings that would help us to steer our nature in the right direction to attain and maintain healthy relationships.

Our nature, meaning our natural instincts, guides us by survival tactics throughout our lives, so we learn to lean on it for most decisions. But what we really need is to be educated to mature wholly; or at least to mature in the areas where our growth requires more than our natural instincts—such as with male cheating.

CHANGING BOYS TO MEN

Everyone knows that young boys need to be taught how to be men. Society has taught us to conquer for millions of years and there's nothing wrong with that, but we also have to learn when to turn that instinct off and use other attributes that ensure the survival of our relationships as we mature from boys into manhood.

The problem is that we males have been left to decide on our own when and where conquering is appropriate, and we tend to use it for everything. Not our faults; it's all we've been taught.

Our antediluvian forefathers used their conquering manhood to get and keep women, and for millenniums men followed their model. We've always thought that if it worked for them, then it will work for us.

But those guys didn't have what we'd consider equal relationships with women. They had hierarchies where women were forced into a supporting role. And because women stayed in their role, there was no need for change. Needless to say, it ain't like it used to be.

Today, males need a new education that guides them in how to have relationships and at the top of the lesson plan is learning how not to cheat. And since education plays an integral role in our socialization, it should also play a role in breeding males to stop cheating.

It's obvious that young males do not possess the natural attributes to navigate or negotiate faithful relationships. So we end up using the only skills that we've learned to survive. Clearly the skills needed for achieving higher education, competing, hunting and physical combat won't work when we're faced with the need to make healthy relationships and that's why we've found ourselves in trouble.

We grow into adults that are on survival auto-drive, never realizing that our relationships are set up for failure because we don't have what it takes to build them.

And there you have it...without the necessary education, men continue to cheat simply because they don't know how not to.

HOW TO MAKE FAITHFUL MALES

Since the formative years is when we teach boys to become men, that's also when we should teach them how not to cheat. It's the same with anything else, the information gets well embedded in the soft tissue of our brains, and we are able to use it to conduct ourselves appropriately with our first girlfriends in our teen years and into our adulthood relationships and marriages.

Males are immersed in the basic rudimentary fundamentals for mental growth starting as young as two years old. As we get a little older, youth sports and athletics are used to teach males how to conquer physically. Back in the day sex education classes were also offered in high school to help teach the birds and the bees, but budget cuts in our educational systems everywhere have done away with that, so young males pretty much get what is available through general education and sports until they are adults.

What we should be doing is breeding males with the tools for better relationships and I believe that this education should be provided in general schooling starting in middle school.

As was my case, we males start cheating as early as our first kisses, so learning how not to cheat should be a part of our early comprehensive skills.

There are some traditionalists that say that this is a parent's job, and I don't disagree. But that's in a perfect world. Today's world is so complex that parents have very little time on their hands to breed their children... and in most cases, young people spend more time in school and socializing than they do with their parents. And that's if they have two parents in the home. For those that are in single-parent homes, the task is even tougher.

If you disagree, keep in mind that one out of every two marriages is a victim of infidelity and men are the accused cheater in over half of them. So even if a young male has both parents, the odds are that he will be in a home where his father cheats.

I firmly believe that young males should not have girlfriends until they have been taught the basic "Six Virtues of the New Man" and have the mental maturity to handle the responsibility. That usually occurs around age eighteen.

Understand, I'm not saying that young males shouldn't date; just that they shouldn't have serious relationships before they are educated on learning how not to cheat.

By teaching young males the basic attributes needed to beat cheating early in life, it will enable them to use it to conduct early relationships appropriately as they become adults and desire more committed relationships.

GETTING BACK TO BASICS

Today, our young males learn their relationship skills by watching music videos, movies, video games and from other mediums of entertainment. And we wonder why they grow up to cheat…these unrestricted forms of information use misogyny to form young males into men that are guaranteed to over indulge and feel they are entitled to what they want, whenever and however they want it.

A male that cheats lacks a fundamental attribute that tells him, "Stop—wrong way!" Without building an internal voice and consequence mechanism, these guys will continue to fail to learn from their cheating and are less likely to ever change.

But with new training, we can create a new beginning to rid our futures of cheating forever.

These principles are the blueprint to perfecting the ability to have and maintain committed and faithful relationships.

There is more on these principles at www.MakingTheNew Man.com.

How Not to Cheat

In my public speaking, seminar and lectures, I teach males all over the world how not to cheat through a new set of basic principles that include:

Modern social skills: Making the New Man

Conquering and nurturing: Balancing Your Good Guy and Bad Boy

Relationship ethics: Understanding Today's Woman

Building an internal voice: Developing Self-Honesty

Building a consequence mechanism: Right and Wrong are Dead

Defining cheating, monogamy and polyamory: Learning New Monogamy

CONVERSATION #2:

Good Guy vs. Bad Boy

I'd invited Ray J to continue the dialogue about cheating and how to become a new man. My goal was to keep him on course and that was already proving to be a task in and of itself because there was so much information in his head that he'd never told anyone before.

That's how it is with most cheaters...the truth gets thrown into the back of their minds because they are too busy perfecting ways to hide it. But I was determined to get him focused on getting the basic elements.

We'd had a good kick-off conversation and he was excited to talk more about becoming a new man. So it was time to get into his actual cheating and particularly how it all started.

So I asked him to think back to the earliest recollection he had of cheating and how it all began.

Here's what happened.

RAY J: I can't help but wonder why my existence has revolved around females. For as long as I can remember, it has been about them—or should I say, it's been about getting them.

It started when I was about sixteen years old. I had a girlfriend my age but an older woman took a special interest in me and showed me what women liked; and I was eager to learn how to give it to them to keep them around. That's what has always kept 'em coming—my skills to give them what they like, so to speak.

I'm not going to front: Having a name helps, but even before I became a public figure, I was consumed by the thought of having crazy amounts of decadence and that also meant lots of women. And as I got older, that desire turned into a thirst for more and more.

So, when fame hit, the desire escalated into an uncontrollable urge. All of a sudden I got access to more money and women than I ever imagined—my life became an exercise in gaining material things and beautiful, sexy women were all right there at my disposal. "Living the Life," as I like to call it, was no longer a dream or an ambition; it became a reality—mine for the taking.

Before long, my obsession for women took over and one woman was more like an appetizer than a satisfying meal. They came in waves and I welcomed them all.

My hook was simple: I found that women liked a bad boy, a guy with swag, wildness and a taste for trouble. There's no denying it. You don't see too many of the so-called good guys with the hottest women, do you?

The truth is every guy has a good and bad boy inside him. As a kid I was always getting into trouble, for one thing or another, and looking back, it was the training ground for what I later became.

When I really got comfortable with myself and learned women like a guy with a rough edge, it was easy to let the bad boy side of me take over because it was already a big part of my personality. And it really took over.

It's not easy to admit now, as I look at my life, but I have done it all—from pouring champagne all over women's asses while partying, to having some of the most notorious relationships in popular culture. I basically swagged it out so much that people expect it from me.

But that was one side of me; not the total me. There is a good guy side to me that, as I mature, really wants to be seen. In the past, he would stick his head out every now and then—but the response from women wasn't motivating.

More than that, I still felt like having one woman was not enough to hold my attention. Many times I tried to re-create the rush that I got from my excessive behavior and womanizing when I had a serious relationship, but it never seemed to last. So, eventually the bad boy always took over again, and before I realized it, it seemed that I was more bad than good.

And to make it worse, the more bad I was, the more women wanted me.

So, as much as a part of me wanted something more, I eventually gave in to my wilder side.

That's how my bad boy image was born.

And the bad boy has continued to attract women at a crazy rate, even though I want to be a new man, but I don't know how to do that yet.

I often feel like I'm cursed, and that I will have to be a bad boy for life. I try to work myself into allowing the good guy to come out more often; that's why I got a serious girlfriend. I felt like it would help make me be monogamous, but I always end up being pulled into the bad.

Take for instance a few nights ago. I had to host this party at this club in L.A. So I kissed my girl goodbye and told her not to wait up for me; it was one of those nights where I needed to get it in. So I hit the party with these two beautiful models. They were the type of women you'd see on a fashion runway in Milan or Paris. Tall and exotic with a lot of attitude—the exact kind of girls that a bad boy can have a really good time with, if you know what I mean.

As is the norm with me, we spent the night sipping champagne and having a good time. When it was time for me to jump things off, the DJ put on one of my records and I took the mic to really get the party started. As I was beginning to speak, this girl in the crowd caught my attention. She had the most sincere eyes I'd ever seen. Her look was totally different than the models I was hanging out with. She wasn't Hollywood slick. She was much more authentic, with a sort of Bohemian look.

Once I wrapped up my flow, the party got bananas. So I made my way over to her and invited her to the VIP where it was chill enough to hopefully get to know her a little bit. I took her hand and we walked through the crowd; truthfully, it was hard carving through the maze of attentive women— one more beautiful than the next. But there was something special about this particular girl that made me want to know more.

When we hit the VIP, I immediately poured her a glass of champagne to relax the mood and we started to talk. She told me her name was Nicole. She was very reserved and almost withdrawn from the wild club environment.

I was conflicted. I couldn't figure out if I should give her the bad boy or the good guy. So, instead of letting it happen naturally, I tried a little of both to see which guy she would respond to. My model friends noticed that I was giving Nicole mad attention and so they jumped in, pushing me to get up and dance with them. They were all over me, and each other. It was clear they wanted the bad boy, so I gave it to them as Nicole watched with a grin of surprise.

As the models and I had our little ménage thing poppin' off, my assistant stepped in to remind me that I had a flight to catch to Las Vegas for another party. It was one of those crazy nights where anything goes, so I decided to fly private. A part of me—the good rational side—said it was not wise to drop 10Gs on a private plane for a one-hour flight from L.A. to Vegas. But the bad boy side of me wanted all the perks that go along with flossing in a private jet, so I didn't give money a second thought. Plus, the promoter was paying me 20Gs to come host the party.

And I figured if this girl was into me, then she'd be into my lifestyle, which was always fast and furious. Private planes, limos, champagne, high-rise hotel suites. Dropping ten or fifteen grand over a weekend was the only way to do it. I didn't know any other way and I didn't want it any other way.

So I invited her to Vegas and made it clear that the other two women were also gonna be with me. I was testing her so I went at her straight-up, bad-boy style. If she wanted to roll, she had to roll with everything that came with rolling with me.

To my surprise, she agreed to come along. She said she understood the scenario and was interested in getting to know me better.

See what I mean—Bad boy wins again!

The party from the club continued in the SUV on our way to the airport runway. The vehicle was large enough for us to maneuver and, of course, it was equipped with champagne that flowed like water down a river. It was no-holds-barred partying.

We arrived and climbed the stairs to the private jet, which was banging. It had all of the leather and marble that I prefer and an assortment of music and lighting to set the mood for mile-high fun—virtually a flying nightclub.

The pilot welcomed me by name and the attendants showed the girls where an assortment of vodkas and champagnes were chilling for our immediate consumption.

Just then the good guy stuck his head out and suggested I use the time on the one-hour flight to get to know Nicole, but the party atmosphere took to new heights as soon as we hit the air. We were getting chopped and screwed—30,000 feet above the earth. Talk about being on a high…it got so steamy with the models that the sixty minutes zipped by and before I knew it, we were landing in Vegas and I hadn't learned anything more about Nicole. And if you've ever been to Las Vegas, you know that it is not the place to try to get to know someone better.

We took another tinted-out SUV to the hotel on The Strip and made our way upstairs to the penthouse suite. I've seen my share of high-priced Las Vegas suites, but this one was the sexiest. It was huge, with floor-to-ceiling windows that revealed the sparkling Vegas light view overlooking the city, two Jacuzzis and enough luxury goods, food and drink to lure any bad boy into more trouble. And there was a big, inviting bed.

By that time, I noticed that Nicole seemed to be getting a little uncomfortable with the atmosphere. So I invited the ladies to a party in the club downstairs that I was hosting and they couldn't wait to get going…we all piled into the private elevator and I was finally able to steal a couple of moments of conversation with Nicole. But I could see that she wanted more time alone to get to know me.

Unfortunately, that wasn't gonna happen because the party we walked into was packed to capacity. The space was seriously swagged out! Complete with a crazy sound system, flashing lights and stripper poles. And, of course, there were girls everywhere, a literal wall-to-wall array of sexy. I was like a shark in a sea of fish—plus, I had Nicole and the models along for the ride.

With the party in full effect, I found myself walking through the club with the girls I'd come with tightly in tote. But once I made it to the VIP, I met two new girls that wanted my attention and because it's all about the ladies, I gave it to them. These girls were not shy about their desire to have fun in Vegas and told me that they wanted their fun to be with me.

The good guy inside of me tried to remind me that I had a girlfriend at the crib, but his voice was weak like he was off in a corner in the fetal position. So since I never really thought I'd stay with my girlfriend forever, I figured why not hang out with Nicole, who was patiently waiting to spend time with me. For all I knew, she could have been the one.

But the two new girls were so tempting that the bad boy burst out even more. And, as so many times before, I gave into him, and invited the girls upstairs to my suite and they quickly accepted. I thought: Do I really wanna leave this party with Nicole here by herself, or stay and try to get to know her? I didn't want to give in to my urges but I didn't do anything to prevent them, either.

Those inner good guy thoughts were there but they weren't enough to prevent me from getting into the elevator to head upstairs. When we got to the suite, we wasted no time getting our own private party started, and I quickly tuned out the thoughts of Nicole by herself at the party.

As soon as we got upstairs, we peeled out of our clothes and slid into the Jacuzzi. And let's just say that the bubbles were popping and the sexy began. It was a whirlwind of sexual energy and straight-up debauchery.

When the bubbles were all gone, we took the excitement to the bedroom with confidence that what happens in Vegas, stays in Vegas.

But as soon as the sex was over, I wanted out of there, with the quickness. I couldn't get them their clothes fast enough, so I could get back downstairs and hopefully find Nicole. But the girls had more fun in mind and wanted to keep our private party going. It was weird; here I had two gorgeous girls that wanted me all night, but as soon as I skeeted, I wanted to leave.

Instead of staying and continuing the hot sex with two women, I felt relieved to be done with them. The truth is that this was not the first time that I've felt the need to bounce right after meaningless sex; and to keep it real, I felt disappointed that I couldn't resist the temptation to be bad in the first place.

To make the situation worse, the girls tried really hard to convince me not to leave. As crazy as it may sound, I really want to get to being the good guy, but the harder I try, the more I'm pushed to be bad.

So, you tell me, Maxwell...what's that about?

MAXWELL'S NOTES } **FELLAS**

Meaningless sex is usually a momentary fix to a deeper need. Everyone loves sex, or at least everyone that I know. But you create an imbalance when you have more meaningless sex than meaningful sex. This is at the core of why we feel the urge to leave once meaningless sex is over; the temporary fix has no lasting effect and we immediately need to find deeper fulfillment. That fulfillment may be felt in the attraction we feel toward someone who represents our core values, or with someone who challenges us to be our true selves.

Being our true selves means being well rounded in both our Good Guy and Bad Boy traits and that makes it vitally important to establish a balance between the voices of both the good and bad to become a complete man. After all, you can't always be the bad boy running around town getting into trouble, but to be the good guy all the time would be boring and that isn't enticing to women, either. Making the New Man is about creating equal parts good guy and bad boy and understanding the appropriate time for both.

To create the perfect balance between the two, you need to develop the good guy's voice into one equal to the bad boy's more aggressive voice. The good guy is usually less assertive and may need to build his voice and swagger in small doses and that requires practice. Expecting him to stand up against the bad boy when you're faced with an opportunity for a ménage à trois, probably isn't the best time to get started building his voice.

A modern approach to building it can come by talking to different types of women on line via sites like Facebook, because they have no preconceived idea of your bad boy side (and this way you don't have to use your real name.)

Start by creating a dialogue through the good guy's voice and interests to engage them. Say only the things that the good guy wants to say and be assertive in his voice. Keep in mind that you're online and no one knows you, so there are no expectations placed on you to be bad.

Keep a record of the things that different women respond to positively. Having this dialogue regularly will build the good guy's confidence and as he receives positive affirmation that he is being heard, he will become stronger and more assertive. Then you can begin to use the things that have worked online in your general dialogue—especially when you are faced with the bad boy's opposition.

Growth takes time, so be patient with your inner good guy. And while you give him time to become of equal prowess to the bad boy, remember that being the New Man is all about balance. Cultivating both the good guy and the bad boy ensures that you have complete self-awareness to aid in your ability to forego meaningless distractions and attract more fulfilling relationships. Ultimately, it makes it possible for you to attract the woman you really want...and FYI, they don't usually come in pairs.

MAXWELL'S NOTES } **LADIES**

I f a guy gets up immediately after sex, take that to mean he isn't feeling you! It's as simple as that. You may think that because he doesn't leave immediately, then I'm wrong. But I am not. It's not about leaving right after sex; it's about his need to distance himself from the intimacy following the act of sex, so that it stays purely physical.

For instance, if he starts making calls, begins sending text messages or gets up to take a shower or even brush his teeth, this means he's only a few minutes away from being out of the door.

Look at it like this: When a guy jumps up right after sex to brush his teeth, what he's really doing is brushing you off of him. To put it bluntly, he's eliminating the taste of you or washing you away. It's the same premise for taking a shower; he's washing you down the drain with the water.

The truth is that if a guy is really feeling you, he will want to have a connection with you that will last after the sexual act. He will desire more intimate time with you via talking, holding you or falling asleep with you. Those are all signs that he's actually into you and not just the sex.

Remember, a man that is feeling you wants to keep your smell and taste for as long as possible, and having some level of intimacy after the act demonstrates that.

The Wrong Day to Cheat

T he question of how far is too far, even when it comes to cheating, may never be answered. But it's obvious that there is a line that no man should ever cross with himself. The real question that must be asked is what makes a man cheat so badly that even he can't believe he's gone to such an extreme?

The void left by the lack of relationship development for males has pushed many a man to sink to the lowest levels of ethics with very little concern or regard for the consequences to come; not to leave off the consequences that such actions have on women.

The following conversation between Ray J and me is the perfect example of the uncontrolled lust and lies that ruin relationships and cause a man to lose himself in deceit.

RAY J: For years KK and I had a great sex life. There was more to our relationship, but the majority of it was about our wild and extreme sexual chemistry.

She was a straight freak who was down to do whatever, whenever and that seriously hypnotized me. There are certain things that a woman can do to hypnotize a man and KK knew them all. We were buck-wild; we would get sexual at any time and then she would do certain things that most women just don't seem to do. Case in point, she had a very special way of waking me up in the morning, if you know what I mean. And then after, I'd go to the bathroom to get my day started and she'd have toothpaste on my tooth-brush and fresh towels waiting. I would be like, damn, this girl is no joke.

On top of that, I never had to shop for myself. She'd take my AMEX black card and take care of what I needed, without me even asking. I swear she must have gone into my closet one day because she knew all my sizes. I'm talking shoes, socks, underwear and suits, without ever asking me what size I was. She had it locked in so everything looked and fit perfect!

It got to the point where when I went out, she would choose my entire wardrobe. I didn't have to lift a finger!

She also made sure that everything was sexy. There was always a panty fashion show for me to see which pair of panties I wanted her to wear, just before we'd go out. And that was on the regular.

I'm telling you—all that mixed with wild and freaky sex makes a man feel like he owns the world. I'd get up and get my hustle on because the sex was guaranteed. For a while it was very exciting, but ultimately, you know what they say: sex doesn't cure a bad relationship.

To be honest, the whole thing started off wrong. We'd known each other for a while before we dated and there was a mutual attraction, but she was married. So I wasn't really trying to push up on her. That was until she let me know she wanted to get with me. And once I realized that she was interested, I wanted it. I mean, what man wouldn't? But little did I know that this decision was the beginning of my loss of respect for both her and me.

She left her husband for me as soon as we started having sex, and things between us got intense really fast. After that, I felt obligated to be with her. Plus, the sex was so bananas that before I even realized it, I got trapped in it…a serious addiction!

We were like animals; sexually free to try anything and we did. It wasn't long before our nonstop sexual activities made me want more and more, but not just with her. My sexual appetite got turned up more than it had ever been before, even with other women. Partly because I suspected that KK was cheating on me, but I was so caught up in my own cheating that I didn't care. Like I said, I had no respect for her or for myself, so it really didn't matter.

I'm not saying that I didn't care for her because I did. Trust me, the way to a man's heart isn't through his stomach, as the old saying goes; it's through sex.

I've gotta give it to her, she was smart; she put it on me right at the perfect time. That first thirty days seemed to put me in a trance. And the wilder the sex, the more my feelings got stronger, and then my suspicions about her cheating started to bother me to the point where I couldn't focus on business. So I used sex with other women to dull the pain and ease my conscience.

That didn't work for very long and the cheating led to distrust and jealousy. After a while, we got caught up in the emotional attachment of being with each other, and the fun that kept us going went away. One day I looked up and realized that I was stuck in a two-year relationship and I couldn't get out.

It got worse and worse!

We started to fight once she couldn't deal with the distrust anymore, so she started going to extremes to monitor my behavior. I was definitely out there, but she literally thought I was cheating with every girl I ran across.

Whenever I'd have to go somewhere, she wanted to know where I was at all times and that caused me to want to cheat even more. For me, I didn't care so much what she did because I didn't respect her, and as long as I was getting mine in, I was fine.

She started watching me so close that I had to go to extremes to hide my cheating from her. It got so crazy that I started to think she even tapped my phone—really tapped it like the police do to criminals.

For the longest time I couldn't understand how she always knew where I was going and who I was gonna be with. As a cheater you always keep your phone game tight. But every time a girl would call or leave me a voicemail, KK seemed to know about it—sometimes even before I could get to the message.

Every time I thought I was getting away with seeing a girl behind her back, I'd get a call from her, drilling me about where I was and who I was with. She'd say that she had some friend of a friend who told her that she saw me with a girl or some phony excuse like that. She knew all the girls' names and where we were gonna meet up...it would trip me out. I was like, damn, KK knows everyone.

I later came to believe she must have been checking my phone and had been using it to keep tabs on me for some time. If that's not crazy, then I don't know what is.

Then I met Risa; she was the perfect woman for my situation. From the start she told me straight up that she understood that I had a girlfriend, but she didn't care and we could keep things between us on the low.

She was a little older and more mature than KK, so I wasn't worried about getting caught because she wasn't trying to get caught up, either.

She was a career woman that was all about making money. Nothing turns me on more than a woman that likes to have sex and make money.

"I want to fuck you and help you do deals," she would tell me.

After I heard that, I couldn't help but want to make it happen. It got to a point where I felt like I had to smash it; I couldn't hold out anymore.

So when an opportunity came for me to do some out-of-town business, I used it to arrange a little rendezvous with Risa.

It was October and I had been trying to get with Risa for almost three months. Because KK was watching me like a hawk, I never had the chance to really get alone with Risa like I really wanted to.

So to set it up, I told KK that I'd be going out of town for a couple of days and would come back on the evening of her birthday. But I really wanted to get in early and go smash Risa down and then go home, in time to sing "Happy Birthday" to KK.

Cheating on KK's birthday was sinking low, but like I said, I didn't have the respect to keep me honest nor did I really ever consider the consequences.

So I let Risa know my plan and we agreed that she'd pick me up from the airport when I got in from my flight back to L.A.

All the way back on the five-hour flight from New York, I was thinking about what I wanted to do to Risa. And at the same time, I was figuring out how I would make sure that I could save enough energy to keep going with KK that night because we were sure to do big things in the bedroom for her birthday. Fortunately for me, stamina has never been my problem.

"Ding," the overhead ring alerted us that we could get up from our seats to get our bags and exit the plane. I was so deep in thought that I hadn't even noticed we'd landed.

I immediately turned my phone on and grabbed my bag to leave. But before I even made it to the airplane door, my phone started blowing up with voicemails and text messages.

It was KK and she was pissed!

"I know you're back in L.A., you piece of shit! You're cheating on me with that bitch and you got caught. I don't ever want to see or talk to you again. It's over!" she said.

By the sound of her voice, it was clear that she was hurt and really meant what she said. We'd played the break-up game many times before because of cheating, but this time sounded different.

I tried calling her back but her phone was off. So I sent a bunch of text messages but she didn't respond. Finally I gave up and accepted what I'd known from the beginning was our inevitable breakup.

Honestly, I felt bad. Even a cheater knows that there's a line that you don't cross, and I had crossed it. My inner good guy tried steering me into deep thought about what I did wrong and what I could do differently in the future.

That's when the bad boy inside of me jumped in and said hold up, she was also cheating from jump street, so forget that; let's go enjoy ourselves with Risa and worry about the rest later.

As usual, my bad boy's voice was much stronger than the good guy's, so I listened to it and made my way to the gate where Risa would be waiting to pick me up.

When I got there, she was curbside with the top down on her Benz. And by the sexy outfit she was wearing, I knew that she was ready and willing to get it in.

I told her what happened and because she was so sly herself, she said, "Don't worry about it. I got you, poppa."

Her words eased my tension a bit and helped me remember why I'd crossed the line in the first place: it was to have sex with Risa. For a second I wondered if it would be worth the damage that had been caused, but by that time my inner good guy was totally muted, so sex was really all that I wanted to think about.

Immediately, we started going at it in the car on the way to her apartment. Kissing, licking and playing with each other until we were both ready to tear each other's clothes off. I was so tempted to have her pull over and go at it right there in the car with the top down that we barely made it to her house. When we finally got to her driveway, she grabbed me and we kept it going all the way inside. It was like the animal in me had taken over and she was 100 percent with it.

Inside, I threw her on the bed and she pulled me on top of her...a big performance was about to go down. When I say big performance, I mean big over-the-top sex, and she didn't disappoint.

It was fantastic, to say the least!

An hour later, we were laying there, taking it all in and she offered me the opportunity to stay the night. But my mind had shifted to getting to my own crib and putting the KK issue to rest. I really wasn't sure if I should go back; after all, it was KK's birthday and I had had sex with another woman.

But my inner bad boy was still pumped up and he let me know he wasn't having it. *You're the man and she has to deal with it*, his voice said. After all, she wasn't perfect in the relationship either.

But for the first time I started to feel like it wasn't worth it. I decided that I wasn't gonna stay away, whether I was the blame or not.

Risa agreed to drop me off, but I could tell she was disappointed. She seemed to think that the issue with KK was her way into a more serious relationship with me.

I was tripping. I thought she really just wanted to have sex with me; that's all I really wanted at the time. I was sure that she realized that she was the casual-sex girl, but I was wrong.

It seemed that the good girl side of her, which every female has inside, wanted more and the great sex we'd had began to trigger those emotions.

But somehow I recognized that I couldn't go from a cheating relationship to a relationship that enabled me to cheat.

At that point I realized that as much as I thought I was doing the playing, I was really the one caught up in the games. Both sides playing the middle—Me!

I went back to KK and even though it was basically over at that point, we worked it out. The truth is, I really wanted to leave the relationship after the encounter with Risa, but I felt like I should make it up to KK, and stop cheating.

That was until KK had a falling-out with my sister involving money. And I finally saw that our cheating was merely a symptom of a deeper issue with self-esteem. We had personally lost all sense of integrity. Seeing that finally put everything in perspective for me and after a long and crazy ride, I broke it off to try and get my head together.

After all my mistakes, I wanted more for my life and realized that some things had to change within me first, if I was ever going to be able to find a woman that I could actually trust.

But it's so hard to stop being the bad boy and attract good girls. I don't know how a guy like me can ever change that.

MAXWELL'S NOTES } FELLAS

So often we men think that when it comes to women, we are in control. Women have allowed us to believe that we run things when the truth is, they do. That is, when it comes to sex.

When men place too much emphasis on the act of sex, it becomes the most powerful thing in our lives and it can even take over our relationships.

Once it does, it governs our happiness and rules our abilities to make healthy decisions. We lose focus of our core values and decline in our professional field. Even the strongest football player's performance suffers once his sexual conquest is gone.

Allowing our integrity to be undermined by sex also causes us to lose respect for ourselves. We may stay engaged in the act of sex with the woman, because sex is the most addictive drug ever known to man, but inside we see ourselves as weak, as we know that we have no control.

The most important attribute in becoming a new man is developing your ability to see consequence.

Clearly, a man who sees the consequences of his actions won't cheat or sleep with a married woman. The consequences are negative and there is absolutely no way that it can be fruitful. Even if you and the woman you cheat with stayed together, the consequence is that you will never trust each other because you both know inside that your foundation was built on a violation of commitment.

You would think that every guy would naturally have this "Consequence

Mechanism," but the truth is most men don't. We generally aren't bred by our parents or society to have it…it's quite the opposite, as a matter of fact.

Those men that have it rise over the pack as consequence helps keep them focused on the big picture of achieving greatness in their lives.

You can start now by using consequence in the areas where you may not see right or wrong. Any time you are faced with a decision or a shade of gray, consider the consequences. You may not feel that being with other women is actually wrong, but the consequence of your woman finding out you've cheated could be devastating for both you and her.

We should all use this method of consideration in our everyday lives. Ask yourself in any situation, can you deal with the consequences. It can help you avoid a parking ticket by not parking in the red, or save your relationship by keeping you from falling to overwhelming temptation.

Your inner bad boy will always push you to betray your core values. Building your consequence mechanism helps you to see what your values truly are, and you can act accordingly.

Keep in mind that using consequence is not about being right or wrong; it's about creating a perfect balance to live responsibly and while we have fun.

And never forget that no great man has achieved his goals without being aware of the consequences of his actions. The last time I checked, great men were still attracting great women.

MAXWELL'S NOTES } **LADIES**

B ecoming a cheater will not help you get or find better men; quite the opposite in fact. If you continue to cheat, you will eventually believe that every man is cheating on you, and consequently, you will automatically cheat to protect yourself in the jungle of cheaters.

Women have natural female instincts that, if combined with knowing the right signs to look for, help them weed out the cheating men. Alternatively, once you become a cheater, your judgment becomes clouded and you begin to make decisions like a man.

Being cheated on is painful and the pain makes us all want to show the other person how it feels. But the consequence of damaging or losing your feminine instincts is too severe. A woman may be able to play the game of men for a while, but she will always lose in the end.

There is an old proverb that says, "What good does it do to gain the world and lose your soul?"

A cheating woman always loses touch with her soul because her relationships are all based on survival and fear. And even when she may seem to have gained fame and fortune from playing men, she's always on guard that sooner or later the world will eventually catch on and see her for what she is.

If a woman really wants to protect herself against her man cheating on her, cheating back won't do it. But there is another alternative.

Once you've caught a man cheating, he will say anything to beat the heat, including promising he'll change. Believe me; I've personally seen it time and time again.

But a man that says he won't cheat anymore because he sees you're angry or hurting, is lying to you. Once you take him back, he has no reason to change his ways.

His promise to stop sounds good and when you're in pain, it's what you need to hear, but make no mistake, he will cheat again.

The key to changing a cheating man is making him prove it. You do this by one easy step, give him a "Time Out" to learn how not to cheat. Yes, like with kids, men need time to consider the consequences for what they've done and learn new skills so it doesn't happen again.

Even if he's truly sorry, if he doesn't have the skills to stop cheating, then he won't be able to. No matter how much he wants to...

Taking a time-out means no sex—not with you or anyone else, of course. He needs to see clearly and men don't see very clearly when sex is involved. He also needs to learn the "Six Virtues of the New Man" that I present in this book.

Taking that time-out isn't only for him; it's also for you. It will give you a chance to heal from the damage that his cheating has caused. If you don't heal, then you will be a ticking time bomb ready to go off at the slightest reminder of his cheating.

It can happen at any moment; something in a movie, television show, song, billboard, or just about anything can cause you to flash back to the moment that he cheated and the relationship is soured.

If he truly wants to change, his actions should change immediately and it shouldn't take long for you to see that he is becoming a new man. He will immediately become more transparent: he shouldn't continue to hide his phone, get strange text messages or have any of the things that were attached to his cheating lifestyle.

Again, if he really wants to be with you and turn his cheating ways around, then he'll become responsible for his actions and go in with you all the way!

Once you've given a man the chance to address his inability to be faithful, you don't owe him, or yourself, anything more. If his old actions persist, then you are obligated to yourself to leave.

But ladies, don't forget that although a new man wants to be responsible, that doesn't necessarily mean he wants to be monogamous. Some men may decide they don't want to be with one woman and prefer to be polyamorous and that's fine too. As long as he's honest about it with you, then he's being responsible.

You may not like it, especially if he's already cheated on you, but don't take it personal. It has nothing to do with you and it's better that you finally know the truth.

If you find yourself in this scenario, look at it this way; once he's gone you'll be free to meet a man that shares your goal of having a committed relationship. And now you know to pay attention to the signs that always reveal when a man has learned how not to cheat.

Six Virtues of the New Man

Change of any kind requires attaining a new set of fundamentals that we can use to achieve our aspirations. For men, making the change from being a cheater also requires an education on how to acquire new fundamentals that can reshape our thinking.

Here is a list of the basic fundamentals every new man will need to make himself a new man.

STRENGTHENING YOUR INTERNAL VOICE (THE GOOD GUY VS THE BAD BOY)

When men find themselves in compromising positions outside of their relationships, it's often because our internal voice or inner good guy is weak and can't be heard.

We all need that little tap on the shoulder every now and then that keeps us from getting into the waters of trouble. Without it, we may find ourselves too deep and before we know it we are drowning.

The internal voice of a new man is the good guy in all men. So often we shut him out and he loses his volume within our day-to-day lives. We can strengthen his voice by giving him power and that means listening to him when he speaks.

Following his guidance regularly will help him speak loudly when it truly counts. Especially for those times when a man's nature tries to overpower his common sense…it can happen to the best of us but when your internal voice is strong, it will provide the clarity and direction that is sure to keep you out of harm's way.

ESTABLISHING YOUR "CONSEQUENCE MECHANISM"

Think of this as a light switch that you flick on when consequence needs to be the main consideration in making a decision. Learning to weigh the outcome of any given situation will help you decide how to proceed.

Acting on impulses can be a deadly habit and that so often is the reason we fall short of our commitments and hurt other people in the process.

As opposed to using the concept of right versus wrong to make decisions, we can use consequence as our barometer for what should be done. As

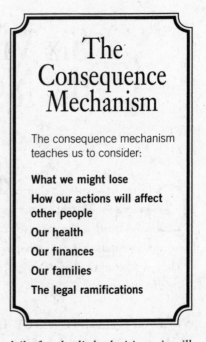

The Consequence Mechanism

The consequence mechanism teaches us to consider:

What we might lose

How our actions will affect other people

Our health

Our finances

Our families

The legal ramifications

we go to our consequence mechanism daily for the little decisions, it will eventually become our guide for the big things—like cheating.

BUILDING SELF-RESTRAINT

No one ever said that change was easy—it takes self-restraint. If you've ever tried to lose weight or change your eating habits, then you know that old habits die hard. They are impossible to change without building self-restraint.

Men learn this in sports and education, but never to apply to relationships. When we apply the same discipline to relationships that we do to learning how to play basketball or golf, then we will naturally restrain ourselves from doing harmful things and work on what helps us get better at our goal.

Like sports, relationships take time and practice to gain skill. As we work on our skills, we have to keep ourselves from the things that take our attention away from our goal. And even when distractions pop up here and there, we have to treat them the same way we treat the bad food for a diet; leave it alone.

KNOWING YOUR LIMITATIONS

As we said in the chapter outlining this issue, why tempt yourself with something you know is your weakness?

If you are trying to lose twenty pounds and you can't resist cheesecake, you would stay away from The Cheesecake Restaurant, right? Don't go there and think you're only gonna order a salad; you are fooling yourself.

Or if you want to quit drinking, you wouldn't hit the neighborhood bar because you think you can hang out and only drink water. That's how you end up drunk and have to start all over again.

The same principle applies to staying faithful in a relationship. Steering clear of the things that we know are overpowering until we have built up our internal voices and learned to use the consequence mechanism successfully is essential to staying faithful.

If you use Facebook or Twitter and get enticed by the pretty girls, then cancel your membership until you can handle it. If you stay dedicated to the things here, you will be able to do all of the things you love to do without the burden of them controlling you.

Remember, pride comes before a fall; don't overestimate what you can handle—know your limits.

BE HONEST WITH YOURSELF

Once a man has built up his internal voice, he has to learn to submit to it. That starts with the acceptance that just because we're men doesn't mean that it's our birthright to have as many women as we want, when we want and how we want. "Pimpin' ain't pimpin' no more." It's important to stay up with the times we live in, and in the modern world, that sort of thinking is outdated.

That doesn't mean we have to get into relationship styles that don't fit us, either. No one can force a man into monogamy and there is nothing wrong with you if it's not your thing. If you have practiced and conquered the virtues here, and decided you want to be with one person, then go for it. But if you feel that you will be most happy in polyamory, then by all means, you should have it. Either way is fine, as long as you keep it real with yourself and anyone you choose to get involved with.

Understand that there is a fine line between being a player and a predator. The latter is only suitable when you are up front, honest and transparent about your desire to be with more than one woman. Trust me, women would much rather know where you stand so that they can make an informed decision to be with you or not.

Becoming a new man starts with being honest with yourself and once you know exactly what you want, you can offer that to someone else.

BECOME A THINKING MAN
"You can teach people what to think and make them dependent, or you can teach people how to think and make them independent thinkers."
—Maxwell Billieon

History has given us many great thinkers. Aristotle and MLK were men who utilized their brains to shape, guide and create new ways of thinking that birthed new cultures.

Somehow the skill of deciphering and processing information to make rational decisions has almost disappeared from our world at large, and not thinking ahead has become cool.

A thinking man understands that there is a consequence to all of his actions. It's not an issue of right or wrong anymore; we must accept that we can't use our natural instincts to guide us in relationships anymore.

By thinking through the consequences, we can become better equipped to deal with the temptations and obstacles that we as men are presented with in our relationships.

EXERCISE YOUR VIRTUES
Begin to view your daily thinking as a sport...understanding that to become great at any sport it takes time and practice. You don't go shooting

three-pointers or even free-throws...you must stand at the line and practice every aspect of your shot.

As you drive, work, play, eat and take involvement in every other daily activity you find yourself in, think about the consequences that surround your daily decisions. Leave no stone unturned...look underneath all of them to decipher what would happen for each of your choice decisions.

Try not to look at the decisions or the outcome as right or wrong. See them as consequences that you can or cannot live with and base the outcome on how it affects you and others. Letting go of right and wrong and accepting consequence is guaranteed to aid you in building character for the challenging times where your natural instincts try to take over.

Although your life gets hectic, write down notes where you can of consequences and decisions you've been faced with and come back to them regularly to see your growth. What you will find is that once consequence becomes dominant in your daily thinking, your demons will become quiet and as in the movie "A Beautiful Mind," you will be able to walk by them and smile.

CONVERSATION #4:

Life Imitating Art

S o many men use life as a copy of our favorite fantasies. From the time we are boys we pattern ourselves after the fictional characters we wish we could be. As we mature we move on to copy some well-known playboy that appears to have the ultimate bachelor lifestyle. The problem is that those types of guys are only really fly in the movies. In real life they have problems, some even more than the average guy. Because the truth is, you can only play forever in the world of make-believe.

The following conversation with Ray J shows how easy it is for men to stray in relationships and allow themselves to get lost in the fantasy of having a cheater's paradise.

RAY J: "When is it gonna blow up?" I'd asked myself a thousand times reference to a sex scandal that was about to happen with my name attache

It was scary because my career was on the line. I thought it was literally as I saw it. I was also nervous about what would happen to my personal I had a girlfriend and really couldn't imagine what everybody would of me once it all came down. At the time, I thought my life and might be over because you can't be respected once you go into a world that involves sex. No more work means no more money. It wa because no one had ever been a part of a sex scandal and come successfully.

After all, I had been the brother of America's sweetheart and on network television. I didn't want my problems to taint my family's reputation or brand. And as for me, I remember thinking, *Damn, I won't even be able to get into a club after the shit hits the fan.*

I was on the phone with a friend who was telling me that I was crazy for letting myself get caught up in such a compromising situation. But by then it was way too late and I couldn't really stop it, so I had to move on and start thinking about what I could do to help my future—no matter what happened.

It was a Friday afternoon and I was scheduled to head out to the Bahamas for an appearance with a friend who was a well-known and respected singer, and I had just come from picking up my wardrobe for the warm weather trip when I got her call.

"Ray, what's this I heard about a sex scandal with you? You are crazy… I love you and all, but I can't be down with a guy doing this," she said. I couldn't even be mad at her; I understood. But I was really thinking that I couldn't believe that it had finally hit the fan. If she knew about it, then it was a reality and there was no going back.

Once the scandal was public, I expected that my phone would stop ringing forever. My first concern was to protect my family. I was feeling down, to say the least, and I expected that phone call to be the first of many people that would tell me they could no longer deal with me. *This is it*, I thought, *I am sure to be blacklisted and treated like an outcast by the industry forever.*

Buzz! I heard the vibrator on my cell phone alerting me that I had a new message. *"Ray, you gotta hit me back. This thing is off the chain,"* said a message from one of my business associates. I had no idea that his call was just the first and before I knew it, my phone started ringing off the hook with people that I'd never even spoken to before. *"Ray, we gotta hook up!"* It went on and on. I was shocked to say the least. People were really checking for me and that was merely the beginning.

It's a trip. A few minutes before that phone call, I thought my career was over, but for some crazy reason, it was the opposite and actually seemed like my career was taking off. I had somehow made it to a new world that I'd never even dreamt existed and it was just the beginning.

The calls kept on coming in and the invitations started to pile up. I got invited to the hottest parties, clubs and events that the entertainment business has to offer. L.A., New York, Miami, even London was calling… "Ray, we need you to get our party jumping," they would say.

"Okay, wait a minute," as one of my song lyrics says, *is this really happening?* Have you ever seen an actor that is up for an award and obviously doesn't expect to win it? At first they look ready to lose, so when the announcer says their name as the winner, they are really surprised and look like…who—me? That's how I felt, like I'd won some prize I didn't even know I was up for.

What was I to do? I had to take advantage, right? I didn't hesitate to start blowing up the spots. It was like I'd arrived at the gates of the land of over-flowing champagne, fast cars and women.

I'm not bragging because it was all strange and new to me. And as much as I wish I could say I planned this crazy wild life, that's not how it went down. To be honest, I was much more the victim of that success than the architect of it. But I was young and naive, so I was down to partake in it… no plan and no guidance or mentor, I was on my own and ready and willing to get it poppin'.

What do you do when the world has seen you naked and you instantly become a bad boy?

I was already a bad boy at heart, but then everyone wanted me to be one, so I rolled with it. But truthfully, I wasn't just a bad boy and, for the longest time, I had tried to show myself differently, even though I always thought that no one really loves a good guy. So the scandal made everyone place their focus on my bad side, even though there was so much more to me that I wanted to show the world.

I decided to go along with it although I had no idea what was on the other side. Sometimes you have to learn on the job, and believe me, the entertainment business is some very real "on the job training" for everyone!

Before I realized it, I had more money than I'd ever seen. Parties, alcohol, weed and women…every day! It was jumping so much that I had a song about my new lifestyle and a video celebrating it. I looked up and my life had made the media.

I can hear Billieon saying it now: "Ray, don't make your life imitate your art; make your art imitate your life." But that's not what I was doing back then. It was all about my life imitating my art and that's when all the fun, or should I say trouble, really began. Looking at it now, it was clear that my art had really become my life. But I couldn't stop it. You know what they say: you can't stop a moving train, and there was no stopping the Ray J party train; it was in full motion.

"Mo money—mo problems," but I prefer "mo money—mo women," and that's what I wanted, so that's what I got. I don't care what anyone says; as a man, if you have a chance to be Hugh Hefner, then you go for it.

Since I always liked having women around me anyway, once it jumped off, I formed a habit of having two around me at all times. No matter where I went, it became normal to have two girls that were down. Don't let 'em tell you otherwise; every man has wanted to be Hugh Hefner at some point and time in his life. I just happen to get the chance to do it.

It was around that time that things started to take a weird twist in my life. Of course I'd noticed that people looked at me differently since the scandal broke; that comes along with the territory. But I never imagined that I'd literally become a sex object. It was like all people saw in me was sex, and women were no exception.

I had a girlfriend and I was trying to be faithful to her. It was hard enough before, but that got much too difficult because I started attracting more bad girls. You know them bad girls; they send text messages and emails out of the blue with naked photos and invites looking to get it poppin' one way or another.

"*Hi, if you like what you see, then come and see it in person.*" That's the kind of message that makes a man wander off from commitment. Partying, drinking and sex, whatever the pleasure, it was readily available. And because I didn't really think that my girlfriend was gonna be the one in the long run, why not have as many as I could until I found the perfect one?

It didn't take long before I started smashing them down; I couldn't help myself. These girls knew what was up with me but didn't care if I had a woman or was in a relationship and that was all I needed at the time.

You would think that it was just the ladies but guys can be on some other stuff as well.

One day, I took my mother, who was also my manager at the time, to meet this guy who was a new business connection. When we started the meeting, it was very professional and typical. You know, the regular business introductions and hand shaking—nothing out of the ordinary.

After a little business talk, my mother left the room so that we could talk about the creativity of the project and all of a sudden the whole thing shifted into something totally different.

"So, I went out to this club last night and met this freak. She wasn't even tripping on me at all. She was the serious jump-off. You know how we get down, Ray! I bought a few drinks and the next thing I knew, we were back at my crib and she was slobbing me down. The head was intense, playa!" he told me. I was sitting there like, whoa, he straight went in on this personal wild experience.

I had to do a double-take because I couldn't believe what I'd heard. Here was a sixty-five-year-old guy talking to me like a street pimp.

"So, if you want her number, I got you, 'cause if I got it, then I know you gonna knock that pussy out," he went on to say.

Man, you can't imagine how that tripped me out. I wasn't expecting to hear that at all, and with my mom right outside of the door, it made things crazy awkward, to say the least.

Less than a minute later, my mom came back in and she could sense that something had changed with me, so I gave her the look that meant I was ready to bounce.

After we left, she asked me what was up, but I wasn't about to tell my moms the type of stuff the dude was saying. But it was obvious to her that something out of the norm had happened.

Later that same week, I took another meeting with a couple of female investors that I had been introduced to by this girl I was messing with. They appeared to be the typical strong female business types I was used to. We met up in their office conference room and again, it started out fine. Until they had their assistant put on a porn tape while we sat and talked.

It was nuts. It was playing in the background while we talked about investments. I thought, *huhn, how the hell did we get here?!* That made two times in a row that sex had gotten into my professional business, and I thought, *Damn, is this what my life has come to?*

I called the girl that introduced me to them and asked her why in the hell they put porn on. She told me that she had let them know that she and I are friends with privileges and that I was the party king.

"There's a time and place to party and during business ain't it," I told her.

After that, I did my best to re-direct anything in my career that was about sex. But it was too late! It had become obvious that the scandal had a life of its own and I couldn't control it. In fact, it had control of me and was consuming every part of my life.

Before long, I couldn't even have conversations with friends or extended family members without sex becoming a topic. It was annoying that my entire perception had become the physical manifestation of sex. That's how it is when you let the bad boy rule your decisions; you don't have a choice but to accept the consequences.

I learned a serious lesson in consequence then, so I accepted that I was going to have to ride it out, whether I liked it or not—no pun intended!

MAXWELL'S NOTES } FELLAS

Modern men are oversexed!

Our fathers were severely overworked, and today's man is severely oversexed—we are bombarded by a constant barrage of sexual images to occupy both sides of our brains on a daily basis that keep us fantasizing about an imaginary life.

It's the life that celebrities seem to be living and we want it, too. Although few of us will admit it, we pattern our decisions in a manner to get as close to their lifestyles as possible—that's life imitating art.

Generations ago, a man could count on his time at home to be filled with opportunities to get closer to his family and friends. The ultimate goal was to build a better family and a man's overall success was measured by whether or not he could provide for a family. Those that fell short were considered failures. And because media and television had stricter rules, the private times that a man encountered sexual images were treasured moments of fantasy that women understood and allowed.

That's how stars like Marilyn Monroe became famous; they presented the allure of sex that was considered taboo for mainstream viewing.

But today's man faces sex on all fronts. He can't even use his computer to search for basic essential information on the Internet without the suggestion that he should join a porn site, or fight through the pop-up photos of women selling anything geared to capture a man's attention.

To add to that, during a man's daily commute to and from work, every billboard and bus advertisement has the newest lingerie model or sexy socialite selling sex. And if that isn't enough, when he gets to work he is confronted by scores of modern women who have replaced traditional business attire with short skirts and four-inch Christian Louboutins.

That's enough temptation to make any man go crazy!

Consequently, modern man has shifted his focus from reaching for more success, to reaching for more sex and with the most women that he possibly can. He does this believing the more women he has sex with, the closer he will get to a day of fulfillment—the day when he will finally be able to be a monogamous man.

This thinking stems from the teaching that there is a woman that is made just right for him and that if he tries enough women, he will eventually find the perfect mate that will be so incredible, he will lose all desire to have other women.

Yeah right!

Fellas, there is no such woman or number of sexual experiences that will make you faithful. No man has ever had enough sex to make him want to be with one woman for the rest of his life. If you don't believe me, ask Wilt Chamberlain.

Let's face it—no amount of sex is enough sex!

While we chase some elusive number of women, we're avoiding the time we should be learning the skills that it takes to be with one woman, or learning that monogamy isn't for us. But because we spend so many years knee-deep in infidelity, we become afraid of the unknown commitment to monogamy.

No woman or amount of sex will make you monogamous. If you want to have a successful relationship with one woman, then you'll need to learn the skills. Without them, you end up a statistic on a divorce court ledger, so why bother getting committed at all? Point blank, if you wanna grow, you gotta know—how not to cheat.

MAXWELL'S NOTES } **LADIES**

Success isn't easy to attain, so if a man hasn't learned how to use his consequence mechanism, he may use his success to cast a bigger net to catch more women—especially when he's in a monogamous relationship. In fact, that's when a man is most vulnerable to the temptation of having multiple women.

Because so many women want successful men, success gives men a false sense of power and deceptively allows us to believe that women want us, when in fact it's what our success represents—stability.

So don't think that a man is all of a sudden gonna be able to be monogamous when he rises to money, power or fame. The odds are that won't happen and using sex to get his attention won't make him take you serious. Contrary to popular belief, there is no amount of sex that you can give a man that will make him monogamous.

Men are sexually driven creatures except when it comes to monogamy. I'm telling you, show me the hottest woman in the world and I will show you a guy that's tired of having sex with her.

The sexy photos you email and text a guy might get you some attention, but that's not how you get a good man. Not to forget that once you send them, they will float around cyberspace forever without your supervision. So ask yourself, do you really want to take a chance on the man that you marry finding you naked on some web site later in life? Trust me, that won't be good for your relationship.

If you expect for men to consider the consequences to make better decisions, the same must go for you. Getting a faithful and committed man means that you have to stop using sex to get or to keep a man.

If you wanna get wild and sexy that's fine, but consider the consequences before you act or expect to be a victim of them.

Know Your Limitations

If there's one thing I recognized while studying Ray J, it's that most cheating men overestimate their ability to control themselves. When a man hasn't received training in self-control, he thinks he can deal with whatever comes. It doesn't matter how strong the temptation is, he thinks that he has the power to surmount it.

But he will often find that when the temptations arise, he will fall more times than not.

This particular conversation between Ray J and I brought to life the importance of knowing where our limits are before, during and after we've learned how not to cheat.

RAY J: I stepped into the Range Rover ready to leave the club and hit the after-hours and find a brizzle (that's a hot girl) to close out the night right. There were a few dimes inside the club that night but nothing I was really checking for. Plus, I was in a hurry because I needed to piss really bad. The constant flow of champagne and vodka all night had me feeling nice, but in serious need of a bathroom.

I love to party in L.A. but unfortunately, there ain't much open after 2 a.m., and it was almost 2:30 a.m. So I told my driver to hit the nearest gas station so I could take a leak. Fortunately, he knew the area because I was much too faded (that means intoxicated) to find anything—leave off navigate us through the streets of Hollywood.

He was about to pull out of the valet when I heard my buddy and these two females that I had gone to the club with shout out, "Wait for us," as they charged into the backseat of the whip.

You gotta understand something about me. Most females that I hang out with come in twos…that's how it's always been. Usually a girl that I want has a girlfriend that she invites along to have fun and we all end up hanging out. It's pretty much become the regular routine.

These two girls in particular were what I call "Jump-Off Girls." That means they were girls that are just for sex; there can't be anything more between us than that.

"Where are we going next?" one of them asked me.

"I was about to leave you guys and hit the after-hours spot, but first I gotta use the bathroom like crazy," I told them.

My driver pulled off and we immediately started clowning about all the different people in the club, but I was too distracted by the pounding of the streets on my bladder to really take note of any of that.

Finally after a couple of minutes, we pulled up to the pump of one of those twenty-four-hour, mini-mart gas stations.

I tossed my driver my credit card and told him to fill up at the pump as I hopped out and rushed inside trying to hold it the best I could. *Damn*, I thought to myself when I saw the line of three people in front of me that were also there waiting to use the restroom.

But I didn't feel like turning around and looking for somewhere else, so I jumped in line and grabbed one of those social gossip magazines to take my focus away; something else…anything else would do at that point.

Ironically, on the first page that I turned to, there was a picture of me leaving a club faded. I looked at it almost in disbelief that it was me and thought, *this has really gotta stop soon.*

At that moment, this hot, young, tight-bodied exotic girl in a sexy mini-dress ran inside. She was turned up to the maximum. Obviously this girl needed to pee really bad…I mean, really bad!

"I gotta go sooooo bad, oh my God—oh my God," she screamed out with no shame at all.

Since I had moved up to second in line, the good guy inside of me urged me to be a gentleman. So I told her that she could get in front of me to go next. I had calmed down a bit from looking at the magazine, and since she obviously had to go worse than me, I thought she'd be quick and then I could go right in.

"You're gonna let me go in front of you?" she asked me. "Thank you so much. You're such a gentleman," she said, quickly jumping in front of me in line.

I could tell by her eyes that she was as tipsy as I was and had probably just come from the club, too. Even though she was focused on using the bathroom, it was obvious that the liquor she had been drinking had her ready for the night to finally jump-off.

"Thank you so much, and since you are being so nice to me, you'll have to let me repay you for the favor. So whatever you want from me, don't worry, baby, I got you," she said, looking me right in the eyes.

That one comment caused an electrical surge in me and my inner bad boy started to snoop around a little bit to find out exactly what she meant. So as always, I let him test her a bit.

"You got me? Cool, give me your number and maybe later we can hook up and get it poppin'," I told her.

"Later? Shit, we can get it poppin' here," she responded. Hearing that, I couldn't help myself, the Bad Boy was at it again.

Like I said, I was a little faded, so it made it easier for me to move in with no restraint. I digested her comment for a quick second and looked at her thinking, *Okay, I'm gonna push the line.*

"You know what, we can get it poppin' here, if you can handle it," I responded.

"Yea!" she responded back to me with certainty to let me know she wasn't joking.

What was I to do at that point? The temptation was there and way too strong for me not to take advantage of the opportunity. For a second I thought about my girlfriend at home asleep while I was out on the prowl. But she would never do something freaky like this with me and I wouldn't even want her to. The good guy inside of me was trying to remind me of that, but he was way too soft for me to pay attention to.

"Okay, hold on, let me buy some condoms," I told her, pointing out a package of my favorite brand to the cashier who had overheard the entire conversation.

At the perfect time the bathroom became free right then. That was the sign that I needed to do my thing. After that I felt like, *I am supposed to do this; it's way too easy.* Even though the good guy inside of me was still telling me to fall back.

But instead of falling back, I told the cashier that I was gonna go in with the girl and use the bathroom, then bring him the key. He looked at me like he couldn't believe that we were really gonna have sex.

She grabbed the key and I grabbed the condoms and we hit the bathroom together.

When we got inside, she started to do her business. And trying to keep some sense of dignity, I preoccupied myself in the mirror, trying not to look at her sitting on the toilet.

Once she was done, I took my turn. And while I stood there, she started fixing her makeup, but I could feel her waiting behind me in anticipation. In my mind I was still wondering if this girl was really gonna let me hit it right there in the bathroom, so I was also anticipating the next move.

As soon as I finished, I washed my hands and without hesitation we started going in. We didn't even kiss! I put a condom on while she pulled her skirt up and got it poppin' as I'd promised.

On the real, the whole thing was a turn-on…it was like a scene straight out of a *9½ Weeks* movie.

She put her hands on the sink and bent over and from there it was on!

There was no hesitation at all…we both knew we had to hurry because there were other people in line waiting to use the bathroom, so the sex didn't last long. But when you're in the gas station bathroom, it's not supposed to.

It all happened so fast, I didn't even get to really enjoy it. But for me it wasn't about that; it was more about the fast-paced experience of it all—the rush.

Once it was over, we cleaned up and walked out like nothing had happened. I was shocked that this girl actually asked for my phone number.

"I was like no, really, you really expect me to give you my phone number?" She was surprised that I said no.

"Gimme yours," I said.

"Are you gonna call?" she asked me. I wasn't sure what she was expecting to happen but I said yea just to get out of there.

I went to the Rover and hopped in like, "Man, you guys ain't gonna believe what happened—I rocked this girl in the bathroom," I announced.

"What? Get the hell out of here," they said in disbelief.

We went back and forth for a quick second and their disbelief quickly turned into belief.

"Why would Ray lie? That sounds like him," my boy said. Then the two girls actually seemed to get turned on.

"We should do that too, Ray," one of the girls said.

At first I didn't really care about what they said or thought. After all, none of these girls was my girlfriend. That's how I am; when you're not my woman, then I couldn't care less what you think or say…I may say the wildest things to you because I don't care.

But, once I saw how easy it was for them to accept such a wild story from me, I felt less excited about it all. I remember thinking, *is this what people think and expect of me…I'm just some dude that has sex anywhere, anytime? Maybe I am a dog like women say.*

But it's not my fault…the temptation was too strong. I couldn't help myself.

I had to do it, right?

No man would've turned that situation down, whether he has a woman or not. It's a part of who we men are and that's what women have to accept.

It's physically impossible for men to turn sex down. I love having a girlfriend, but as a man, I can't pass up having a sexual experience like that.

Especially because I didn't even go after it—it came to me so I couldn't walk away from it.

So Maxwell, are you gonna tell me that it's possible for a man to turn that down? How is a man supposed to be faithful with that sort of temptation?

MAXWELL'S NOTES } **FELLAS**

What is it about temptation that draws us into it?
The allure of things, places and people that we know aren't good for us is often the aphrodisiac that ignites trouble for men everywhere. And even though we know we are headed into an area of no return, we keep running back to it time and time again, only to fall short to something that we had no business being involved with in the first place.

Not that women don't have their share of falling to temptation; after all, they do cheat as well.

However, men have had a problem dealing with the temptation of women for millenniums, especially when we're enticed by sex.

As a man, I am all too familiar with the feeling that I need to satisfy the desires of the flesh.

So many times I'd battled with the call of my internal bad boy's voice that pushed me toward dark places where I'd be weak.

It's different for women, because they usually fall into temptation after they succumb to the fear that the desires of their hearts will not be fulfilled. Then they become more susceptible to men who disguise their interests with phony concern, which appears to be the support they need. But before they know it, they're engaged in sex with the very man that they thought was interested in their heart.

For men, our problem with falling to temptation is not generally characterized by the needs of our hearts, but more often the needs of our flesh.

Point is, men need sex and most guys will do just about anything to get it!

But when we are focused on being faithful, it's vital that we keep sight of our true level of skill to avoid being caught in the net of overpowering temptation.

Every man has a limit…knowing where your limit is will always keep you out of trouble.

When men are overly confident in our level of resistance, we convince ourselves that we are capable of handling environments or people that can easily become the beautiful distractions that always knock us off-course.

The way you learn to resist temptation is by learning to stay away from it first.

Know your limitations!

It sounds too simple to be true, but it's how the human brain works. We all know our weaknesses: You know that you can't handle being around the nightclubs without going after women, so until you have built up your self-restraint, keep yourself away from those dangerously tempting environments.

Sure, sometimes it's brought to you when you least expect it. So you need to work on developing the ability to deflect it as soon as it gets started.

A great method is to practice deflecting temptation on a daily basis. You probably aren't gonna be able to turn the hot *9½ Weeks* type of girl away when she is feeling freaky, if you haven't practiced.

The stubborn guys will say, why should I? Well, the answer to that is simple: ask yourself why should your girlfriend or wife turn down the guy just like you? You know you wouldn't want that, so that's why you should grow up. And this is how you begin.

Start by deflecting comments with women that don't have anything to do with sex on a daily basis. It's a bit easier to get used to doing it when it's not going to get you laid. As you regularly interact with women, take their comments and bounce them in a different direction, away from any sexual interests of yours. Once you've done it, you should immediately keep it moving. That means move on to another subject or simply exit the room.

Think of it like baseball—3 and out. Well, with women it has to be more like 1 and out…that means one non-sex comment and get out of there. Don't push the line or make additional comments to test the waters. That will always lead you into getting caught in your own web.

Like I said, the key is to keep it moving until it becomes a general practice.

Example: A woman says to a man, "You look good today."

Cheater: "So do you, baby, what's your name?"

Non-Cheater: "Thanks for the compliment and have a nice day."

After that he's out of there, but the cheater is looking for any reason to further engage the temptation.

If you learn to take the comment away from temptation, after a while you'll recognize the exact comments that tempt you, and you'll be able to deflect them with skill and precision.

MAXWELL'S NOTES } LADIES

It's the modern era and you deserve to have the same fun as men do. But equality doesn't mean becoming men.

If a man wants to have sex with you when you've just met him, he doesn't respect you. Men respect a woman that they can't have at their leisure. Giving yourself up to a man immediately makes him feel like you don't have ethics or morals and most guys want a good girl.

He may even like you and have enjoyed the wild sexual experience, but he can't help but wonder if you're like that all the time or have been that way with other guys.

Once you go too far on a whim, you are "The Jump-Off Girl." That means you're only good for sex.

Some women may not want anything more than sex from a guy, and that's fine. Nowadays you do have that option, but don't think that you won't be judged as a jump-off; you will.

So ladies, keep in mind that no man wants used goods...we want to feel special, like we are so great that we brought that bad girl out of you. Not like you bring her out every time you pull up to the gas station pump. We see that promiscuity as being a manly trait and women shouldn't act like men to us.

Understand this point, when you behave like a man, it doesn't mean that we see you as we see ourselves. We have a built-in expectation that you are supposed to act, think and behave differently.

When you betray those innate values, it causes us to think low of you.

Just because you feel like you have the right to have as much sex as a man; or have the right to have it as quick or as fast as a man, doesn't mean we will accept you like a man.

We won't!

Of course our flesh may want the sex right away, but we will only respect you if you act like a lady. Sure, once we've gone down a certain time line with you, then we want the bad girl to come out. But trust and believe that if you give her up at the neighborhood gas station, you won't be getting a follow-up call.

So go ahead and have a good time, enjoy yourself. But take pride in being a lady; it's exactly what we men love about you, even the bad boys.

Learning How
Not to Cheat

"All men are created equal."—This statement from the U.S. Constitution couldn't be more appropriate for cheaters. So, I've written a new universal constitution for cheating that goes like this: "All men are created equal, when it comes to cheating."

Now let me clarify. I'm not saying that all men cheat; that's not true. But I'm saying that all men are equal because we have never been taught how not to cheat as a whole.

I do believe that our wiring for cheating comes from our social breeding. Men aren't bred to cheat, but we are bred to lie. Most men are socially bred to lie to themselves about their true desires and needs when it comes to intimacy.

Notice, I didn't say sex; I said intimacy. That includes sex but also means conversation, spending time together, hanging out, text messages, emails, phone calls, social networking and anything else that involves intimate time.

Cheating can only occur when a man or woman breaches the agreement that has been set with their mate to govern their intimate relationships with other people. If there is no agreement, there is no cheating.

When two people jointly create the rules of their commitment up front, there is no room for confusion or misinterpretation of the agreement. But when we leave the rules to assumption, we often find out that what we assumed would be common sense, wasn't very common at all.

All intimate relationships should have an agreement. That goes for marriages as well as boyfriend and girlfriend relationships. A violation of the agreement with the opposite sex on any level is cheating.

Learning how not to cheat is as simple as keeping the agreement. And in cases where we no longer want to keep them, learning to communicate that to the other person and exiting the relationship will eliminate cheating altogether.

So if it's that simple, why do so many men cheat?

Men cheat because we haven't been taught the basic skills to function in monogamous relationships. Consequently, there are two basic issues that get men into trouble with cheating.

1	**2**
Getting involved in a committed relationship where we are incapable of being faithful either because we haven't learned the skills to be monogamous or refuse to be honest with ourselves about our desire to be polyamorous.	Staying in a committed relationship after we've lost the desire to be committed to someone. We haven't learned the skill of leaving, so instead we stay and cheat.

Some people think that there are other excuses for cheating such as drugs and alcohol, physical violence and getting revenge, but these issues fall under the aforementioned.

When we are taught the skills, we can and will stop cheating.

TAKING THE FIRST STEP

The skill of learning how not to cheat may only seem impossible because for centuries, we have failed to acknowledge the necessary training. Accepting that we have to learn some very basic attributes in order to change is the first step. Once we have done so, we can move toward the next part of the change.

You don't need a Ph.D. to do this—everyone can begin their own personal change from being a cheater by doing the following: STOP LYING!

We've all heard the age-old saying that "the truth shall set you free." This is where we begin to find that consequence outweighs the outdated concept of right vs. wrong.

When I first began to learn how not to cheat, I realized that at the core of all of my cheating was lying. I lied to myself about who I was and what I was capable of, so I lied to women. When I decided to change forever, my journey started with a commitment to being truthful at all times.

First, I accepted that I was a cheater and that I didn't know how to handle being with one woman. I admitted that I was afraid of telling women the truth because I didn't think they'd give me a chance to get whatever it was that I wanted or needed.

LETTING GO OF FEAR

The next step was letting go of my fear and being honest about my interests and agenda with women. Where in the past I would lie to protect myself, I began being honest and stopped worrying about the outcome.

In fact, I was so determined to change that I went to the extreme of talking to women about some of the most uncomfortable stories of my cheating to see if they would accept me in spite of my past.

I was happy to find that most women are more concerned with what you do going forward, than they are with who you were in the past. Fellas, you may be surprised to hear this, but women don't all believe the old "once a cheater, always a cheater."

Remember, with women it's not so much about what you were, as it is about what you are. Women want to believe that we've changed and they are more open to it than we have given them credit for.

CONSIDER THE CONSEQUENCES

Cheating is not only about you and your mate; it also affects relations between the male and female community at large. Every time a guy gets caught cheating, a woman takes the pain back to her village and then spreads the fear throughout the female community. As a jointed community of women and men, that fear becomes widespread and as we see now, it easily becomes an epidemic.

The numbers don't lie—women have caught up to men in cheating because men haven't stopped. For women to continue cheating means a consequence that none of us can bear. That makes it vital that we understand that the consequences of our actions do affect each other.

We all have a choice when it comes to cheating. Basing our decisions on whether we can bear the consequences trumps any opinion on whether cheating is right or wrong. If we consider the consequences before we act, then we can internalize the effect that our actions will have before we make a bad decision.

I can speak personally to the fact that there is no glory or honor in cheating. It is, and should be, considered beneath even the biggest cheater of any age.

DON'T SEND YOUR REPRESENTATIVE

Many people have been made to feel that we must put up a front of being perfect or having more material things than we actually have to get a mate. When we do that, we cheat ourselves out of finding someone that has the same desires as we do.

The key to finding a mate that is right for our personal needs and desires is to be right up front with the real you, so don't send your representative.

It is instinctual for us to put our best foot forward, and there is nothing wrong or dishonest about that in theory. However, it should be your own foot that you put forward—not one, oh say, the size of Shaquille O'Neal's.

If you act like you can be monogamous, then people should rightfully expect that from you in a relationship. Rule No. 1 for that guy is no cheating.

So if monogamy isn't your thing or you have another agenda, then you have to be up front about it. No woman can be herself if she's being tricked into monogamy. And that also goes for tricking yourself into thinking that you can be monogamous. If you haven't learned how, then you can't do it, so don't lie to yourself and consequently, you won't lie to her.

Learning how not to cheat is easily achievable once we learn how to be honest with ourselves. Recognizing that, as much as the physical act of cheating, is a part of the violation of the agreement; the lie precedes the act and is ultimately responsible for the destruction of trust, once the cheating is brought to light.

So, in actuality, once we stop lying to ourselves and to others, we automatically stop cheating.

CONVERSATION #6:

How I Learned Not to Cheat

I t had been a couple of months that Ray J and I had been talking about his cheating. You never really know how someone is handling change until you see it yourself. But I'd heard through a few people in Ray's circle that he was starting to sound different to their surprise. "He is talking about being responsible now," one of them remarked to me.

That was great progress for both he and I, but even though he appeared to have been making great strides, I couldn't help but wonder when he would seriously commit to allowing the things that he was learning to take over, stop cheating on his girlfriend and be able to discover himself without damaging her further.

Then, as cheating men often do, he got himself into another situation that proved to bring all of my teachings to life. You know what they say: "Be careful for what you wish for."

Here's what happened.

RAY J: "I had to learn to hate the old me." That's what Maxwell Billieon said to me the first time I asked him how he learned how not to cheat.

When he first said it, I couldn't understand where he was coming from... I thought he was tripping because I didn't believe that any man could ever be faithful for the rest of his life, because on the real, that sounded like an eternity to me.

"What does that mean; you learned to hate the old you?" I asked him. "Come on, MB, you can't be serious that you hated yourself because you cheated," I added.

"To break cheating, you have to learn to see yourself for what you truly are. The truth is that you function out of ignorance and arrogance just so you can get your way with women and that is unacceptable. Once you make that realization, you can see that you were conditioned to cheat because you were never taught how not to. It's not something that you do because you're a man. If that were the case, then women wouldn't cheat," he replied.

I'd always thought that I was being a man when I cheated. For real, as far as I knew, all men cheated, so I felt like we were all built this way. That's why I didn't know if any man could really ever change. But Maxwell's words made me pause and rethink everything I'd ever known, seen or heard about cheating.

For weeks I tried to figure out how I could learn to hate myself. That didn't exactly sound easy for a guy like me that was used to having women everywhere. And I couldn't see how that was ever gonna change because I really didn't want to stop having my cake and my ice cream, as I like to call it.

One day I was stuck on a long flight and couldn't fall asleep. Usually I take up that time and vibe out to some music, but I remembered that Maxwell had told me that times like that are perfect for self-realization. So as hard as it was, I started writing some things down about myself to see what would come out.

It's a trip; you never really know what you think about yourself until you have to put it on paper. About halfway through my list, I realized that I wasn't really cool with the things I'd written down about myself. Partially because before I started this journey to see if I could stop cheating, I felt like I was the shit. I wasn't really trying to change my whole life or anything. I wanted to see if a man could really stop cheating.

But putting my life on paper showed me that I really had never thought of the consequences of the things I had done in my life. It was hard to admit everything, but I figured, what the hell; no one was looking so I could at least be honest with myself.

I was finally reaching "the age of intellectualism." That's what Maxwell calls the time in all of our lives when we start asking questions about who we are and what we want to be. I had always been on autopilot for as long as I could remember and never worried about the consequences of things before. I'd always been the type of guy where anything goes. But right about that time, something happened that brought me into the reality that MB had talked about.

I was messing around with this girl that had this very hot best friend. They were both so hot that secretly I wanted them both. So I figured, *Why not try?* That made perfect sense to me at the time because like I said, it was anything goes.

One day I hit 'em both up and was like, "What would you guys think about all three of us being together?"

"What do you mean 'together'?" they asked.

"Like girlfriend and boyfriend but as a trio," I said.

They were shocked at first and acted insulted. "You mean you wanna be in a relationship with us both? You must be high, Ray!" one of them said.

"Yea, just like that…I'll move you guys into my crib and we can all have fun together. It's no big deal either way, but we could be on some Hugh Hefner-type fun; living the life if you guys are down. Think about it and let me know—it's all good," I said.

It was one of those days that I was on full tilt, so I wasn't really trippin' on what they thought. Even though I came at them straight up, I have to admit that I doubted it could ever happen. That's why I was surprised when they called me back to say that they were down.

It's on now, I thought. Then I knew I should take advantage of the opportunity right away, so I moved them into my house in L.A., the very next week.

It was like a TV show: they came in and picked rooms and everything. Once they got settled in, we started going hard…it was rotational sex like you've never seen before. Morning sex with one girl, lunchtime with the other and then a ménage à trois for dinner. That first month I was like, forget everyone else, I'm the man!

They jumped right into my lifestyle…we were partying together almost every day. I'd hit a club with them both and other guys would be peeping hard, trying to get tabs on them. But I wouldn't even trip because I was the new Hugh Hef!

One time I came home and it was all dark in the house. So I hit the lights not even expecting anything and to my surprise, they were going at it, right there in the living room. "We started without you because you took too long," they said, looking up at me laughing. I was like, hell yea, this is what every man is wishing for!

It wasn't until the second month that things got weird. All of a sudden they both started acting jealous of the time I'd spend with them individually. I noticed they started saying little comments to me to show that they each wanted to have me alone. It had never dawned on me that almost any woman is going to want more than mere sex after a while.

I was having too much fun so I tried to ignore the jealousy and keep doing my thing. But that didn't work and the relationship between them started to get ugly. They started fighting and arguing over little things like if I bought one of them a purse, I had to buy the other one a purse just because or she'd get pissed. It got so bad that anything that I did with or for one girl, the other one would get jealous and it would cause a fight.

Then one day when I was least expecting it I got a real shock. They'd decided they couldn't share anymore and that I needed to choose one of them to be with. In my head, I was like, *Damn, how am I gonna do that?*

I was selfish and wanted to keep things like they were. So instead of taking it seriously, I refused and figured it would work itself out eventually. That was really how I'd lived my life in every other area and it had seemed to work just fine.

But these girls were best friends and in my selfishness, I didn't see that their relationship was on the edge because I wanted to keep them both. But in my trying to have my cake and my ice cream, they had become rivals and I was too blind to notice. Then, like that, it was over—one of them decided she'd had enough and moved out.

But what messed me up was that they'd broken off their friendship, and it was all because of my selfishness. And, for the first time, what Maxwell had said to me had come to life. I started to truly hate who I was.

At that moment I wanted the carefree guy inside of me that didn't think of the consequences of his actions to be gone—actually, I wanted him dead forever. He was simple-minded and he was causing me distractions. Not just with women, but there were professional things I wanted. But because I was always so focused on getting as many women at any costs, I was suffering in achieving other things that needed my serious focus.

When you're out there getting it poppin' all the time, you don't see what's really going on all around you. I knew then that I could have been even more successful if I'd gotten my personal issues together. It was at that point that I realized exactly what MB meant when he said he'd learned to hate the old guy. I had also learned to hate that guy inside of me, and I finally got serious about changing my life forever.

I remember thinking that there was no way out and that I was cursed to be a cheater forever. It may sound a little dark, but in my mind, I felt like to stop cheating I needed to commit suicide—not to kill myself, but to kill the old guy inside of my head that was causing the real me trouble.

The messed-up thing is that when I would tell people that I was gonna stop cheating and running around, no one believed me. "C'mon, man, that's not you, Ray," they'd say. I thought, *Damn, am I really that messed up?*

So the only thing left for me to do was change everything around me… women, friends and even business associates. I started by doing anything that I could to make the statement that I was determined to become new.

But old habits die hard, and that bad boy inside of me was still pushing. He was much stronger than I thought he'd be and for a while, he did anything to trap me. I'd hear his voice telling me to do something and I almost couldn't resist. I was so addicted to listening to him for all those years that I didn't really have self-control.

It wasn't easy, but little by little, I learned to ignore the bad boy and listen to the other voice inside my head that was much more concerned with consequence.

The hardest thing was when I realized that I needed to break it off with my girlfriend that I had been cheating on. I figured that was the right thing to do; I wasn't capable of being monogamous yet and knew I'd keep cheating until I fully learned how not to. I had always wanted her to ride with me while I tried to learn to be faithful, but that wasn't fair and it was destroying her in the process.

When I told Maxwell, he actually thought it was good. I asked him, "How is me breaking up with her good when I was the one cheating?" He told me that I had become responsible enough to be honest with myself, and being honest with her was what she wanted all along. That meant that change was happening.

I said, "Okay, this better be worth it because it's not like me to let a woman go!"

After that my whole perspective changed. From there it was all about telling any new women that I wasn't ready to be in a relationship and that I was gonna see different women. Keep it real with myself and not overestimate myself to think that I could do it too soon. I didn't really want to be in a committed relationship but had chosen to do it because I wanted a woman to be loyal to me. That's the thing that made me feel safe. But I didn't know how to be loyal to one woman, so I needed to learn that first before I could expect it from someone else.

I can't say that it's been easy and smooth since then. I still get the urges to be in a relationship, but I also wanna keep doing my thing. But I learned that I gotta keep it real with myself because those two things don't go together.

Straight up, I can't say that old school monogamy is for me. I don't know right now if it will ever be my thing. But I do know that I won't get into that kind of relationship again with a woman until I know how to do it.

There have been a lot of crazy times and I still wanna have fun. But now I understand how to keep everything transparent with women and not become a victim of my own desires. In the end, if you're honest with yourself, you can be honest with everyone else and that's all that anyone can ask of you.

Conversation Finale—
The New Man

The beginning of my conversations with Ray J started off as a twisted array of stories that showcased the basic way a cheating man's mind works. Initially, most of his actions had no regard for his effects on women, but then there were some of them that seemed more apologetic and sincere.

As we got going, I felt positive enough that if I'd changed, then he could change as well. But over the weeks of our discussions, my optimism that he would actually stop cheating was hampered by his ambiguity and then I started to doubt. Not because I didn't think he could do it, but I wasn't seeing that the discipline that he needed to change was there.

But as we moved ahead, the realization that his relationships were always within his power to destroy or to make successful began to take shape and eventually, I could see that a thinking man was inside of him.

As we rounded out our journey, he took a look back and his statements finally took on a tone of responsibility that ultimately proved to me that any man can change from being a cheater if he is ready to see the truth.

Here's what he said...

RAY J: It's crazy how I went through this journey of becoming a new man. Once there was a time when I really didn't give a damn about anything. I was a bad boy on the run like the law was out to get me. I was taking down women with the same mentality that a bank robber robs a bank, without care for anyone getting hurt—just get in and get out.

As much as I wanted to change, I fought it for a long time. There are always ups and downs with any change, and I've seen my share of them. But then I got on this journey with Maxwell Billieon to learn "how not to cheat."

Before then I'd always felt like I was entitled to get my way with women. I was the type of guy that thought I didn't need anybody, and that meant I didn't need a woman for anything except sex.

That attitude may sound selfish, but as men, we are kind of taught that's the purpose of women. So if we don't have anyone around to teach us the opposite, and most of us don't, then we grow up thinking this is how it's supposed to be.

No disrespect to women in general, but when I was wildin' out with different women every day, I wasn't finding the wifey type of ladies. I'm sure they were probably there, but all I attracted were the bad girls. So I figured that if I was going to survive in that world, then I had better look out for me and me only, and that's how it was—survival.

When you have that attitude, you don't wanna commit to anything or anyone, especially not a woman. You feel like you should be able to do whatever you want, especially when you're young. I call that being a "bandit."

When you're a bandit, you don't want to have any responsibilities where you really don't have to have them. Even when you have a girlfriend, it's like, so what, it's only temporary. Your goal is to get the world in the palms of your hands and take advantage of everything that you can while you're young. If your girlfriend doesn't like it, then she can raise up and you can easily be with someone else. That sounds crazy, but it's reality for a lot of men; especially those with money or fame.

But that way of thinking leads to becoming an adult that thinks they don't have to compromise for anyone. You break a lot of hearts and lose track of them because you're moving so recklessly.

However, a real man feels responsible for others. You can't only think about yourself all the time—that's really not cool! But again, when you're in that "bandit" state of mind, you don't care about the consequences of your actions. It's almost as though you purposely rebel against any rules just to avoid having to be responsible.

That was the bad boy inside of me...I didn't give a damn! And once I realized that I could make money without leaning on anyone else, nothing else mattered. Money became my woman and we fell in love. I never cheated on her and she never cheated on me. It was all the relationship I needed.

"I don't care what you think; if you can't deal with it, then you can be out," I would tell any girl that would challenge my way of thinking. And there were many of them because you have to keep them in rotation to maintain your sense of power. As soon as one of them tries to tame you, you get rid of her and move on to the next. That's the way it has to be because if you let one of them stay for too long, she may cause you to look at yourself in the mirror.

One day I finally chose to look in the mirror on my own, and I couldn't help but notice that my "I don't give a damn" attitude was also affecting other people. It wasn't only women; it was friends and family as well. For the longest time I didn't think that I was doing anybody wrong; not morally anyway. In my mind I was being forced into cheating by women who couldn't handle me being a man, so I rebelled against any thought of monogamy.

I was never able to be monogamous. I was more the guy who would get into a relationship with a girl as long as I was still free to do my thing. I'd give her enough information to keep her around if I felt she was the loyal type, because loyalty was important to me. I was honest about being a free spirit, but not about how much or how I would do it.

Some of my girlfriends knew that I would have other women around. It wasn't a secret because I wasn't a cheater that put on a front like he didn't have any game going. I didn't have to do that because there was a certain expectation that I would be a bad boy anyway, and that made it easier to do it. They didn't like it but I didn't care. Actually, I thought it was okay as long as I didn't bring it home.

Is that cocky? Sure it is, but that's how I was getting down.

But that gets old, or at least it did to me. How long can you go on just thinking about sex, money, success and excess?

If that's your only focus, then you'll do anything to get it. But if you continue to do people wrong, it kills your own blessings, and the money and success you are so focused on getting will die anyway.

That's how I got to the point in my life where I realized I needed to grow. So I had to accept that the things that have gone wrong in my relationships were my fault because of cheating.

At first when a woman would challenge me, I was like, "Who do you think you are asking me about where I've been or who I've been with? If you don't like it, then I can be with someone else, and so can you." But letting go of that ego trip and realizing that in a relationship, I have to give myself to someone, helped me to change my outlook.

I'm not saying that I'm perfect now because no one is perfect. But I am thankful that I got to go on this roller-coaster ride because it helped me to learn that I wasn't prepared to be 100 percent monogamous.

Now, if I ever get into a serious relationship again, I understand how to do it differently.

Before I was an "Asshole Cheater." That's a cheater who doesn't give a damn. Excuse my bluntness, but I gotta be straight up with you on this one. I knew even if I cheated and got caught, the girl wasn't going anywhere...I could always say something that would make her stay. So ultimately, I didn't give a damn—I was an asshole!

But now I realize that if I fall in love and decide to be with one woman, then she shouldn't be hurt because of my inability to be monogamous. And that means I have to be ready before I do it.

We should all be responsible and learn how not to cheat. If we do slip up, then we shouldn't bring home diseases, babies or other issues to women. I'm not copping out. I'm saying that you should do your thing honestly before you commit and get into a relationship.

But if we somehow ever mess up, we can't allow it to penalize another person. That is what responsibility is about. If you mess up in your life, your mess shouldn't become someone else's mess.

That's why I decided to stop cheating and be honest with myself. I learned my limitations and realized that ultimately I want to be monogamous. So I learned the "Six Virtues of the New Man," and they really changed my life. That change made me want to use my mistakes to help others in hopes that the truth I've told here will help someone else grow so that they don't have to go through the confusion I've gone through.

The stories I've revealed here weren't always easy for me to say and it was even harder to admit what I've done. But I have changed, and if I can, then so can others if they want to. For the first time in my life I'm dedicated to "Making the New Man" and by the end of my journey, I hope that my life will lend to restoring some of the hope that I tore down by cheating.

Thank you for allowing me to be personal and giving me the opportunity to be honest.

Getting a Man Upgrade

O ne of the basic attributes that attract women to cheating guys is their presentation. They look, smell and talk the part so women buy into their persona.

Keeping your relationship interesting means keeping your woman interested. And every woman likes a man that's put together. Just because he doesn't cheat doesn't mean he should lose his edge and swagger. The New Man will find that people will believe that he's changed on the inside, if he also improves his outward appearance. Gone are the days where looking manly meant being sloppy or unpolished...men have become more modern in thinking and a modern woman wants a modernized man.

"I don't have the money to buy expensive things" is no longer an acceptable excuse for looking shabby. Women have found all sorts of ways to stimulate men visually and they expect for men to do the same. It's not difficult to find stylish basics in almost any affordable store, so any man can look as good outside as he's feeling inside.

I've outlined the elements that stylish men around the world use to build their wardrobes. These are the basic essentials that every man should know and have to enhance his lifestyle as a New Man.

Ladies, don't be afraid to take the lead. We men love a woman that can make sure we stay on point. So if your guy doesn't have the skills, teach him. If he can't get it and you can, get him started and expect him to take it from there.

It's time to upgrade!

THE BASICS

HEALTHY MIND AND BODY

As this book rebuilds a healthy mind, we must also keep our bodies healthy. Women love a fit and health-conscious man. After all, we are supposed to be the leaders so they want us to set the pace. We can start by upgrading our eating habits. Getting and staying fit starts with eating.

Traditional men thought meat and potatoes were a man's meal. But as modern men we know that myth isn't true. It's vital that we eat green vegetables daily and reduce our intake of foods that cause high blood pressure and diabetes, like salt and the other things that damage our bodies.

Eating a healthy diet of raw green vegetables like broccoli, green beans, spinach, cucumbers, asparagus, snow peas and a variety of others will keep your alkaline levels up. These foods are also a great way to guard against cancer and Alzheimer's.

From there it's all about working the body. You don't have to become a model or Mr. Muscles. But a general fitness lifestyle can make all the difference in the world; even in the bedroom. Regular exercise is proven to build sexual stamina and that can only help keep a relationship moving in a healthy direction.

We should all exercise a minimum of three days per week on alternating days for a minimum of thirty minutes. As you progress your body will become stronger and crave more and before you know it, you will have a healthy lifestyle.

RAISING YOUR STYLE IQ

In getting a man upgrade, every guy should also have the basic elements of a New Man's wardrobe:

Dress shirt (white, blue, gray; semi-spread and spread collar)

Ties (black, blue, gray; if you're creative, try a bow tie)

Suit (black, navy, gray; keep cuts classy and stay away from trends.)

Jeans (A classic pair of denims in medium blue will work with all seasons.)

Shoes (black and brown; lace-up and loafer; daily wear should be a semi-dress shoe, unless you work in an environment that dictates a uniform; sneakers or casual shoes on the weekend)

Casual shirt (crewneck, V-neck, polo cut; black and white; long and short sleeve)

CUT

Trends are cool for added flavor, but a man's basic wardrobe should fit his physique. Tee-shirts and jeans are an added bonus for those bad boy days. A man's basic essentials should remind him of the perfect woman—classy and fun.

UNDERWEAR

No "Tighty Whities!" Most women don't like men to wear the same type of underwear that kids wear. So the old Batman- or Superman-inspired drawers are out and so is wearing any pair until the waistband begins to fall off. Those may be comfortable, but you look like an '80s *Porky's* movie when it's time to get it in.

For a modern comfortable option, opt for the boxer brief half or full cut. Regular boxers are also fine and traditionally picked by men because they are cheaper. But keep in mind that most underwear for men are purchased by women and they generally prefer the boxer brief.

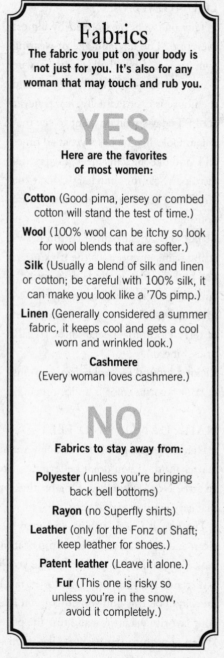

Fabrics

The fabric you put on your body is not just for you. It's also for any woman that may touch and rub you.

YES

Here are the favorites of most women:

Cotton (Good pima, jersey or combed cotton will stand the test of time.)

Wool (100% wool can be itchy so look for wool blends that are softer.)

Silk (Usually a blend of silk and linen or cotton; be careful with 100% silk, it can make you look like a '70s pimp.)

Linen (Generally considered a summer fabric, it keeps cool and gets a cool worn and wrinkled look.)

Cashmere
(Every woman loves cashmere.)

NO

Fabrics to stay away from:

Polyester (unless you're bringing back bell bottoms)

Rayon (no Superfly shirts)

Leather (only for the Fonz or Shaft; keep leather for shoes.)

Patent leather (Leave it alone.)

Fur (This one is risky so unless you're in the snow, avoid it completely.)

LOUNGEWEAR

This one gets overlooked by almost everyone. The day and age of wearing gym sweats, basketball shorts, a wife beater or your old football jersey around the house is over (actually, it was never cool.) Today's women want to see that a man looks like he has style at all times and not like he cuts beef all day (no disrespect to the butcher). Don't be afraid to chill out in something more polished.

At home (A great pair of cotton drawstring pants always does the trick.)

For bed (Cotton is the easiest option); you can go traditional or sporty

After shower (Keep it basic with cotton or terry-cloth; for special times, try silk or cashmere.)

Kicking around (A cool pair of slip-ons in your favorite color is a nice touch.)

Patterns

Solids
(Keep most of your wardrobe simple and solid patterns and over time it will save you money because class never goes out of style.)

Tweed
(used for winter months to add variety to a blazer or slacks)

Gingham
(great for button-ups or dress shirts)

Herringbone
(a traditional favorite of gentlemen)

Polka dots
(best kept to basic color ties and handkerchiefs)

HAIR, HANDS AND FEET

Hair styles range based on a few variables. Age, race and shape of head matter most. If you don't believe me, have you ever seen a white guy with an afro? Not a good look. Or a brother with a straight perm? Well, I'm sure that says enough right there.

The hair is the first thing a woman sees after your face. Keep your style clean and polished and stay on top of it (no pun intended) so that you never look like you need a haircut, or like you just got one.

If trends are your thing, go for it, but keep it updated and fresh. One of the ways you can find something you like is to do tear sheets. Grab one of your favorite magazines and tear the pages out with the hair styles you like. When you go to the barber, take them with you and he or she should be able to help you get the style you're wanting to achieve much easier than if you try to describe it to them.

It's no big deal for men today to take care of their hands and feet. In fact, most women prefer it. It's not even considered metrosexual anymore; it's being clean. Some guys are still shy about it because it may seem like it's for women only. But fellas, believe me, nothing feels better than a fresh pair of hands and feet. Ask your favorite wide receiver.

However, if getting your hands and feet tailored seems too much, grab a complete home nail kit. They come with hand and feet clippers, cuticle trimmer, cuticle pusher and file. Try to do it yourself as regular as possible. Once a week is optimal but twice a month should be sufficient unless your job or daily activities demand that you do more upkeep.

> **SIDE NOTE:**
> Fellas, stop biting your fingernails and cuticles. Remember, we're not animals anymore! For the natural look, splurge a bit and get them buffed. And forget about nail polish; that's reserved for women and pimps only!

BASIC NO-NOS

Never wear white (sport socks) with dress shoes or casual slacks.

Never wear more than three buttons on your suit or sport jacket, unless you're 6'8" or taller and even then, that's a lot of suit.

Never let your jacket or blazer cover your palms. Crop the sleeves a minimum of a half an inch from the base of your thumb.

The only bling that is classic are earrings and they should be kept to a half-karat (if you've got it like that). Fake jewelry is better kept to no jewelry.

Get a real watch—don't buy knock-offs; everyone can tell it's fake.

Re-sole or re-heel shoes when the back begins to tilt (if that's not possible, then there are plenty of less fortunate people that could use the benefit of your old shoes.)

Don't shave or wax unwanted body hair (invest in a personal trimmer for nose, ears, eyebrows, face, etc.)

> **SIDE NOTE:**
> There are aberrations to every rule so switch it up at your own discretion.

SPEAKING AND LANGUAGE SKILLS

Words are the food for thought…getting ahead in life isn't so much about what you say, but the way in which you say it.

I've noticed that women don't necessarily respond to what a man says, but more so how he says it. Even telling the truth is an art form. When a man cheats, he has to perfect the way he lies to appear believable. Well, telling the truth should involve the same panache.

Every man should take pride in his method of speech. Although modern schools fail to teach this basic essential, a new man should take the time to speak clearly and slowly; it helps to ensure that he is understood.

It's also good to go with what you're comfortable with. Have you ever been around someone that tries to use a vocabulary that they aren't familiar with? It's embarrassing.

Keep it simple. You don't want to sound like the old Damon Wayans character from *In Living Color*.

There is a time and place for everything and that even includes cursing. Using foul language is considered poor taste most of the time, but it can come in handy if you use it at the right moments, even with a woman. During sex or foreplay, some women like to talk straight. That's a good time to let the bad boy do his thing and it can be just the thing that a woman needs to take it to the next level.

SIDE NOTE:
Never use curse words in an argument with a woman. It only makes her an opponent.

BE A DOMESTIC MAN

Most guys that I know have very few domestic attributes. They grew up in a world where their parents neglected to teach them the basic elements of self-survival within a domestic environment.

I was fortunate that I was taught to wash clothes, dishes, iron and do the other basic domestic duties that are necessary to keep a house running smoothly. That teaching is the polar opposite ideal for most men…by neglecting to teach them to be domestic, their parents were, in effect, teaching them that being domestic isn't necessary for a man and that it is a woman's job.

But in today's world, women are leaving the home to take up corporate desk jobs in the workplace. Consequently, men are finding themselves at home frustrated that they cannot perform the duties to keep the home going.

Fellas, here are some basic essentials for any New Man to make a part of his arsenal:

Laundry (color match; white only, blacks separate and colors together, or simply read the box of laundry detergent.)

Ironing (Check out my blog for exact example.)

Making the bed (Check out my blog for exact example.)

Vacuuming (Should be done at least once a week depending on foot traffic in the home.)

Cooking (This doesn't require talent, only the ability to follow directions. Don't be afraid to pick up a recipe or two for the days when your woman is too tired to cook.)

PART III

The Real Destruction
of Women

Recently, while I was on www.MakingTheNewMan.com, a female subscriber posted a question asking me why I thought men wanted to destroy women. At first, I thought I'd encountered a confrontational woman. I get that every now and then when I speak about the issue of cheating. Needless to say, her question caught me by surprise, so I responded and asked her what she meant and she sent me this message.

"Destroying women seems like it's the in thing to do for men today. How else do you as a man explain the amount of guys that are using their fame, money and power to cheat on their women in ways that always tear them down when the cheating comes out?"

I prepared a video response to her about the issue and after I recorded it, I continued to think about her concerns. It wasn't hard for me to understand how women could look at the men of today and see our actions as destructive to them. The stats about cheating men don't lie, and no one seems to be paying any attention to the negative impact that constantly seeing men cheating all over television and the Internet is having on the psyche of women.

Popular culture has brought the fate of women to the bright lights of media, where their destruction is put on Front Street almost daily. It has gotten to a point where we're no longer shocked to see familiar faces caught cheating.

Last year alone there were more than five celebrity men caught in cheating scandals. Among them all, Arnold Schwarzenegger has to surely be one of the most notorious and infamous of recent accounts.

The famed movie star and former governor got himself caught up in one of 2011's worse cheating stories. It is unbelievable for America that Mr. "I'll be back" fathered a child by one of his house staff members and chose to keep it a secret from his wife for years, all while he was governor of California.

How Arnold discreetly pulled it off is still a mystery; considering that next to President Obama he is the most famous politician in America.

The story went global and shocked the world as it watched yet another American man's wild exploits unashamedly tear down one of America's most adored women. His wife, Maria Shriver, has been left smoldering in the afterburn while beauty shops and gossip magazines talk about her destruction as though she is dead. A case of "Another one bites the dust" for man.

But we can't single Arnold out; after all, his is a story all too familiar throughout the American male community. A community filled with centuries of irresponsible men that often demonstrate that the destruction of women, often lays in the actions of the men. And no action has devastated more women in history than male cheating.

In 2010, actress Sandra Bullock won her first Academy Award, which many people thought would catapult her career to new heights. Unfortunately, it was the infidelity of her husband, Jesse James, the famed bad boy of the motorcycle world, that sent her fame sky-high. After a microscope was placed over his cheating, Sandra's life became media take-out. Desperate and ostracized, Jesse's public efforts to atone for his long list of infidelities fell on America's deaf ears, as the public made him out to be a veritable Charles Manson-like killer of monogamy.

Not long before Jesse, the most popular golfer in history, Tiger Woods, was brought under the same magnifying lens after his wife revealed to the court of popular opinion that he'd had a long line of mistresses that he'd kept in a stable of promiscuity. The best golfer to ever play the game, Tiger was all but forced to apologize to his mistresses on national television, accepting the moniker of being a sex addict. And as if that weren't debilitating enough, his wife filed for divorce and it was rumored that she'd be granted $750 million in their split.

Even future football Hall of Famer Brett Favre got caught having inappropriate relations behind his wife's back with a female team employee via the Internet and text messages. And still, after all of that, the stories keep piling up. It's as if men don't watch television or read the news to see what will happen once they're caught cheating.

Although it may seem like it, this type of behavior is nothing new. In fact, it's old news, but the Internet takes the news to a whole new level of exploitation. As soon as a man is caught, he's on the front page of Yahoo.

But that's not even the scary part. It's more that after enduring these infidelities for millenniums, women are seeking their own form of justice. That justice is they are cheating back and doing it just as much as men.

But that sort of revenge does not carry with it man's atonement or the advancement of the sexes and it will certainly not prevent men from continuing to cheat. You can see that from looking at the men we've named here.

In all fairness, I can't argue against women wanting to exact revenge on cheating men. But as a jointed community of men and women, that will hurt us both. It's time that we all take responsibility to change this problem. After all, none of the men we've named cheated alone. They all had willing female participants…mistresses who knew these men were in committed relationships but acted to conspire in the cheating. The truth is that some women don't give a damn, and it's always been that way.

So any women that want to blame men for their destruction, have to point the finger at these enabling women as well. They play just as strong of a role in the destruction of women as men do.

The truth is that women also need to check themselves before they wreck themselves. Remember, ladies, no man can cheat without a woman enabling him.

How Women
Enable Cheating

What is a "Cheating Enabler"? Simply put, this is a woman who makes it possible for a man to cheat. Some women do it through denial or ignoring that their man is cheating, and others do it by allowing a man to cheat with them. That is where we find that most women participate in the act of cheating.

Surely we cannot assume that all men lie to their mistresses or concubines or that all women involved in affairs are simply ignorant victims of some evil man's plot to have sex or intimacy with more than one woman.

In fact, a recent poll shows that 65 percent of women over the age of twenty-five who admitted to being involved with cheaters knew it. That's a large number of women who enable men to cheat. It's a married or committed woman's worst nightmare and it's the major concern of women everywhere. This problem has plagued women for so long that it's finally become an epidemic in the female community, and there is an increasing amount of women that admit to doing it.

Why is it that some women make themselves readily available to cheating men?

Some women say they do it because they've lost hope that there are any men that won't cheat, so why shouldn't they? They will find any excuse to get what makes them feel wanted, or what they feel they deserve without consideration for the consequences of their actions, much like the men that they cheat with.

One woman told me about a married man she had been sleeping with for a year... "He told me that he was separated from his wife and was going to get a divorce," she said as the disclaimer for her actions. To which I replied, "Separated is not divorced!"

Still, she went on and on about how it was different for her than it was for other women that sleep with married men and that he was a good guy who would not have lied.

What? Are you serious? How many times have we heard that one before?

First up, ladies, "I am separated" is the oldest line in the book. It's the oldest excuse that married men use. Secondly, as I said, separated is not divorced or emotionally available. Clearly this woman had no sense of self-worth before she entered into that arrangement. If she had, she would've required proof that this married man was eligible, but she never even thought to ask for it, she told me.

She could have demanded to see his divorce filing papers, listen to him and his attorney discuss the divorce, or even speak with the so-called ex-wife. But she didn't because deep inside, she didn't want to find out the truth. A cheating enabler rarely wants to face the truth about their actions.

What's even worse is that like with most cheating enablers, in the long run, she was the one who got dumped. Yep, because she desired a deeper commitment than any married man can give, she decided to see other men and then the guy dumped her.

Later, she found out that, as I'd said, he was still involved in his marriage. It took all of that for her to admit that she knew it was wrong, but that she accepted it because she needed the attention of men. And for so many women like her, any attention will do.

Ladies, please get this: as long as there is a supply of women who will enable men to cheat, there will be a demand for them...it's the law of supply and demand at its best example.

But what about the tons of women who have been tricked by a cheater? Is the issue the same for them? For those women, please allow me to state the following: seldom does a cheater not show you what they are, if you pay attention to the signs. Usually, you get hit in the face by little rocks before the big boulder comes crashing down on your head.

Women ignore the little rocks, some mistakenly, but many do so intentionally because of their lack of self-worth. And like the woman I spoke of that chose to accept the married man's excuse that he was getting a divorce without demanding proof, women who ignore the signs are also cheating enablers.

Why would anyone put themselves in an arrangement where they are guaranteed to lose? Think about it; if you knew you would never win the lottery, not a chance of it, would you still play? Probably not… yet every day, women continue to invest themselves in relationships that can never be fruitful.

Time and time again I've heard enabling women put the blame on men. They claim that men are all liars, but these are the very women that believe they are in love with a man that they know is lying to them. I do not mean to sound insensitive, but in my opinion, a relationship based on love must be inspired by truth. So if your mate can't be truthful with you, then who doesn't love who?

I'm not a psychologist, but it doesn't take one to see this fact.

Cheating enablers usually act on impulse to avoid making well-informed decisions. That's what makes it possible for them to ignore their own true self-worth, allowing themselves to be used for what they believe is their own benefit. Again, this is why when they get involved with a man, they avoid asking him the necessary questions to find out if he's really available. Or if they find out he does have a mate, they accept any ridiculous excuse he has for stepping outside of his relationship without requiring any validation or proof that it's true.

So what makes a woman become a cheating enabler?

Perhaps it's the potential of being alone; age; fear of not finding anyone better; losing the sex; having a father who cheated; or other determinates that may create a list so long, it takes counseling to root its true core. The bottom line is self-esteem and that must be recognized to stop the enabling cycle.

HOW TO STOP ENABLING CHEATING

Sometimes facing our truth head-on is challenging, but in my experience, improving self-esteem often requires dealing with issues that may extend as far back as childhood, and that can take time. However, many of us need to make a change sooner than later; after all, at some point in time, we must all stop sugarcoating our problems and face them. I believe that the quickest way to the center of any issue is in a straight line.

I have found that with the admission of who we truly are, along with the acceptance of where we truly are in our lives, we can work small miracles for self-esteem. Even in therapy, we can't expect any type of psychological counseling to get to the root of an issue if we aren't first ready to admit and accept that there is an issue.

Again, I'm a realist, not a psychologist. And being a realist means that I have to be honest with myself first and foremost at all times. Accepting who we are is as real as it gets. It forces us to take responsibility for our growth and to see that we have choices in our lives. Cheating is among those choices, as is allowing someone to use you to cheat. Understanding that you have a choice to be used or to be happy is huge, because no one has ever been truly happy being used.

Women today have become less sensitive about being used. They contend that they are somehow getting something out of it as well. Whereas in earlier generations it was seen as a sign of weakness, modern women are more apt to play the game of cheating so that they don't have to be alone. But being alone by choice is strength and should not carry any shame or guilt.

I have a saying that goes like this: "We attract to us what we are, especially when we make the decision to accept what we are not."

Accepting your choice to stop enabling gives you the ability to move into the self-realization and discovery of who you are truly meant to be. No woman is meant to be used by a man. Accepting this may also mean going through some pain if you're involved with a cheater. But never fear; the laws of nature are at work and you can rest assure that in due time, once you stop enabling, you will attract what you truly are…a new woman for a new man.

How to Tell
If You're a Cheating Enabler

Go to your computer and open up Word. If you don't have a computer,
then it's okay to go old school with a pen and paper.
List the names of the people that you've dated over the last five years
and for each one of them, answer these questions:

Did he regularly turn his phone off when he was with you?

Did he have real photos of another woman or other women on his phone, computer, etc.?

Did he keep you removed from his family or friends?

Did he say that he was separated or getting a divorce soon or in the future?

Did he keep you away from his house, or only come to meet you at your home or hotels?

Did he tell you that he wasn't available on the weekends?

Did he only see you during one particular time of day regularly?

Did he tell you that he had to go out of town regularly and/or leave town for extended periods without calling or contacting you?

If you answered yes to two or more of these questions,
then the odds are you were or are enabling a cheater.

WHAT TO DO NEXT

As an adult, it's important to remember that no one, including your parents, is to blame for your decisions. Personal progress sometimes requires us to bear the responsibility of our indiscretions and to move forward on our own two feet.

If you have been a cheating enabler, allow yourself the time to forgive yourself. Remember that you now have the choice to use earlier decisions as a guide to better decision-making in the future. Focus yourself on your future and do not falter in moving forward according to the new direction that you want for yourself. Write it down and make it clear.

Remember that you have a choice to create new actions based on your desire to have true commitment with someone that is right for you and you alone.

The 30-Day Rule

What do we men consider to be too soon for a woman to have sex with us? A guy can have sex anytime, but why is a woman still considered dirty, or a slut, if she has sex with a man within the first few times they go out, or for that matter, on the first date?

The concept that a woman should keep her "nookie" to herself until a man becomes serious with her is as old as any belief on the planet. It seems to have stemmed from religious beliefs mostly, but it has found its way into popular thinking and spread itself across the common thought of dating and social etiquette.

Should the modern woman still live by this rule? If she wants to get a man that respects her, then the answer is still YES! But there is a slight shift in today's thinking that has created more freedom for modern women and it goes something like this:

When a woman makes a man wait for the nookie for more than thirty days, he puts his focus on doing whatever he has to do to get it. After thirty days, he feels like he's made an investment so he has to get it. Often he loses focus on building the relationship with her and almost completely shifts his focus to the time that he will finally get it.

So when he finally does get it, he loses interest in the woman immediately. Why? Because she made him wait too long for the nookie...the truth is that there is a time frame that women have where they can keep a man interested in building a relationship and not just in getting sex.

For men, getting a woman is like hunting for a rare prize. When a man hunts, he sets a trap to catch his prey, but after a while, if he feels like it will take him a long time to catch it, he will shift his focus to catching something else that can be caught easier. But as hunters do, a man will still leave his trap set to catch the first prize, in case it finally comes around. But he focuses on what he can get immediately. That's the nature of the hunter.

If today's women want to keep men interested in getting into committed relationships, they must apply what I call "the 30-day rule."

WHAT IS THE 30-DAY RULE?

Popular belief is that women are more emotionally attached to sex than men are. Not true; men can be as emotionally attached to sex when a woman gives it to us at the right time.

For most men, that time is during the first thirty days of getting to know a woman. That's when a woman has our full attention, interest and testosterone riled up. When sex is mixed in at the right time, it forms a chemical charge inside of a man that causes a reaction with our dopamine.

During my research for this book, I learned about dopamine from a well-respected clinical psychologist. Dopamine is a natural drug of sorts that we humans have. It's some serious stuff! Some doctors refer to it as the "pleasure potion." In fact, it's so lethal that it's the chemical that the drug cocaine affects in the human body. Both women and men have it, but males are said to have about 500 percent more of it than women, and it is the signal that tells us we are experiencing extreme pleasure.

When a man's head and body are aligned in pleasure, he tells himself that if he continues to be with the woman that he's experiencing the feeling with, then he will be able to continue to feel elation if he stays with her. Ever wonder why some women always get a good-looking or successful man, even though they may not look like they would be able to? It's because she doped him up! That means she gave him the nookie at the right time and got his dopamine jumping.

HOW DO YOU KNOW WHEN IT'S THE RIGHT TIME?

Here's the key part to the rule. If a man gets it too soon, then he tells himself the woman is easy and she probably gives her nookie the same way to any man. That cheapens the experience for a man and consequently, we don't feel special.

Understand this point: men need to feel special. We want to feel like whatever a woman is doing, she's doing because of us—not because she is easy to any man that gives her the right attention.

Usually, if two people are dating regularly, somewhere around the third or fourth date is the perfect time to catch a man at his most vulnerable state of mind. It's usually the time where we are equally invested into getting the woman and getting the nookie. So, if two people are dating about once a week, which in my opinion, is the minimum time that a man should be putting in if he's really trying to get to know a woman, then within a month's time, they should be getting together for the third or fourth date and that's when the connection is most powerful.

Don't believe me? Well, a recent survey showed that most couples that got married within the first three years of their relationship had sex within the first thirty days. That's proof that if you wanna lock a man down— knock a man down by the end of thirty days!

HOW DO YOU KNOW IF IT'S JUST GONNA BE SEX?

Nothing is guaranteed when it comes to sex, especially if that's all a man wants from a woman. Ladies, don't get upset because there is nothing wrong with that...in fact, sex may be the only thing you want from him, so the 30-Day Rule is the perfect way to get it all on the table.

Asking a man what his intentions are is a great way to break the ice on the subject. And a woman shouldn't be shy about revealing her intentions, either. But she should never discuss when or how long it will be before she will have sex. That ruins it for men and we wait until that time runs out. If a woman wants to know early if she will have something more than sex, then she must put the 30-Day Rule in effect as soon as possible.

The key is for both people to be 100 percent honest about their intentions early, and that means they should discuss it within the first thirty days so neither of them waste their time trying to form something more than sex if it isn't possible.

Communicating intentions works especially to a woman's benefit within the first thirty days because that's when most guys send in their representative to try and convince a woman that they are the perfect man. But that's a dead end and can be a deceptive trick to get the nookie.

If two people are honest about what they want and what they are capable of giving during the first thirty days, they have more of a chance of making it through the next cycle of getting to know each other.

WILL A MAN CHEAT BECAUSE HE'S HAD TO WAIT LONGER THAN THIRTY DAYS?

Not all men are the same, but I can say that generally a man that only wants sex probably won't stay very long once he sees that a woman is going to make him wait for the nookie. The dangerous guy is the one that will wait to get to the nookie even though he isn't interested in building a commitment or excited about the woman anymore. Those guys are usually the ones that will cheat because they walk themselves into a committed relationship just to get the nookie. When they look up, they are trapped in it and the only way out is to cheat or flee.

Again, discussing intentions up front will help to alleviate any concerns a woman has. Ultimately, if there's a sense that someone isn't being honest about their intentions, then you can use your consequence mechanism to decide if you want to continue. There's nothing wrong with being precautious, and remember, no one has to go forward if it doesn't feel right.

The Nookie Opportunity

The No. 1 excuse that men use to cheat on their mates and to stray from their committed relationships is sex. Understand that I say "excuse" because sexual issues aren't a reason to cheat. As I have said here, there is no "reason" to cheat or to stray when you have learned how not to.

However, there are reasons to leave a relationship. And yes, sex or the lack of healthy sex is most definitely a reason to leave a relationship.

Statistics show that for most men, the issues that they face with women are as follows:

- Refusal to have sex
- Lack of sexual frequency
- Sexual betrayal or cheating
- No sexual chemistry
- Inability to have sex

Of them all, the simple act of a woman telling a man "no" is the biggest complaint of men everywhere. It is also at the root of why many men say they lose interest in their commitments and begin to stray mentally, which is always the first step to physical cheating.

Once a man enters into a committed relationship, he naturally feels a sense of entitlement to sex. This "entitlement" emboldens him to expect that sex within the relationship will be readily available to him. In fact, having "sex on tap" is one of the main reasons that men say they get into committed relationships.

As soon as we men make the decision to commit, our desire for sharing in a variety of sexual experiences with our mates will automatically increase, and we will, of course, want the sexual frequency to increase as well.

Because women do not have the same internal drivers to sex as men do, generally men want it more often. Although many women today say that a lack of sex is also a major determinate of whether they will stay committed to a relationship, the majority of relationship stats still show men with the stronger sexual desire.

Millions of women complain that the male sense of sexual entitlement or appetite often proves to be too emotionally and physically demanding of them over time. Women naturally desire to incorporate other emotional elements into the relationship when they feel that a man belongs to them. If that isn't nurtured, they may begin to take away the man's sexual freedoms within the relationship to attain what they need by saying no to his sexual advancements.

But it's important to recognize that while no means no for women, by nature of a man being fully committed to one woman, for us NO stands for "Nookie Opportunity."

That means that every open or available opportunity for sex should be fulfilled with sex. In our thinking we believe that our commitment to the relationship or to a woman creates a right of receipt and that the relationship presents us with the opportunity for guaranteed sex or the Nookie Opportunity.

This belief and stance that we deserve sex can create confusion for unsuspecting women who may see our bold demands as archaic and unbridled machismo to get whatever we want—when we want it. However, it's quite the opposite; it's our way of showing that we are 100 percent into the woman and feel that she is ours.

With all this going on behind the scenes, it's vital that women know that when it comes to keeping a man from cheating, a woman should never tell a man "no" when it comes to sex...it is the single most deflating word that men can hear in a relationship. When we are told "no," it causes us to resent women and puts a divide between us.

In instances where a woman may not want to have sex, in lieu of telling a man no, it's better to tell him "yes, but later." Adding whatever pet or nickname to the end, such as "baby" or "honey," will create a more welcoming feeling for him, and it ensures he will continue to make advancements at more appropriate times.

And it doesn't have to necessarily mean a woman saying no. "Oh, okay, why not?" or any other sort of delayed or unenthusiastic response will cause a man to feel like he is being denied what is rightfully his. In addition, it's equally beneficial to stay away from using words like "maybe" or "possibly" in reference to giving us sex. These type of words and responses serve to cause us to feel like we have to get permission to have sex with you, and that is confusing as we already believe that sex is freely ours for the taking.

Ladies, maybe you can think of sex this way. Instead of giving him permission, give him a license to have it.

When we have a license to have, use or do something, we can do it freely almost anytime we choose. Commitment or marriage for us is a license to sex. Again, men feel a sense of entitlement to sex when they commit to one partner. Telling him no is a strong contradiction to that and provokes us to flee the commitment to find something or someone more inclined to give us full usage of this license.

Let me clarify this viewpoint. When you get a driver's license, you have the freedom to drive a car at will. It isn't until you have broken some sort of law that your privileges are taken away. This is exactly how we men see sex. Unless there is some serious offense to a woman, such as cheating, there is no reason why our license should be suspended or revoked.

The bottom line is men don't want permission to have sex; we want a license to have intimacy with our committed partner anytime and anywhere… no, that's not too much to ask. That's what a license is.

This does not mean that women don't have the exact same rights to intimacy or "sex on tap." We are partners in the relationship so look at it like this. The same laws apply to women as to men.

Fellas, women today are evolving sexually and with their enhanced positions in the work place and new roles in the home, they are desiring sex more on a man's level. More than ever we are hearing about men that don't want as much intimacy as women. Sure, the numbers are small, but it is a factor that must be considered.

So for all purposes, both men and women have the same rights to the Nookie Opportunity. For women that means they can use the Nookie Opportunity for their benefit when desired. And you better believe it; the man has to be willing to provide the same access as he demands. After all, no man wants to find out that his woman has strayed because he wasn't having sex—that is the ultimate embarrassment for any man on the planet.

HOW MUCH SEX SHOULD KEEP A MAN FROM STRAYING?

There is no such thing as a man having enough sex to keep him from straying. But not having enough sex is an issue and as much as I hate to have to admit it, we men aren't all the same in our frequency levels.

For some guys, once a week is enough, and for others, it may be every day. I disagree with psychologists that say that one or the other is healthy. That isn't fair. No psychological approach can dictate what should or shouldn't be normal for a couple by any means other than a traditional look at who we have been as humans; not necessarily who we can be when we are well armed with new information.

That is why communication is the key to it all. Most couples never discuss what they want in a sexual relationship. The determination of how much the man should have is based on how much the woman is willing to give. That puts her in control of it and leaves the man to have to find unique ways to continue getting it over the long term.

However, as adults, we must discuss the exact level of intimacy that is needed without judging what is healthy. Women tend to make the judgment that "all a man wants is sex" if he desires it more than she thinks is appropriate for what she's willing to give. But that's unfair and is a huge cause of men fleeing.

Ladies, try to look beyond the act of sex and see the man's desire to be faithful to you is being expressed through his desire for sex with you. He wants to have sex with you and you only and is showcasing his commitment to doing that by his advancements. If you judge that desire in assumption that it's not enough or it's too much, you may take away his desire for you altogether.

Another way to look at it is that we are taking all of the sexual energy that we would normally use to cheat on you with multiple women and placing it all on you. That is a lot of energy coming your way and it needs to be received and cultivated so that it continues to evolve for long-term commitment.

When a faithful man feels that he is welcome to have his woman at his leisure, he has the license he needs to be creative in ways that he will use his license; that creative mindset can be cultivated by the woman telling him what she likes and how she likes it. And because he knows that he has no restrictions, he stays focused on the relationship.

Some women feel that if a man is getting sex too often or if it's too easy, then he will lose interest and cheat—but that's not true for a faithful man. Remember, his goal is to preserve the commitment so he isn't looking for reasons or excuses to stray—he's looking for reasons to stay.

Determining how much sex he needs has to be based on each couple sitting down and coming up with what is best for them based on their needs. Nothing is too little and nothing is too much. As they say, "just do you." But no matter what, don't judge his desire either way.

WILL A MAN STRAY EVEN IF HE GETS THE NOOKIE OPPORTUNITY?

Lastly, sex isn't the be-all to a relationship. It is the main factor considered for most men, but without the other things such as nurturing and commitment, a man will still stray. We now have to let go of the old concept that if you keep a man happy in bed, he will stay. Not true! But if you don't keep him happy in bed, then he will stray; that's almost guaranteed.

But you also have to take into consideration that today we men are more complex than our fathers and are more in touch with our feelings. Sure, we want sex to the maximum amount physically allowable, but we also need the emotional attachment that creates the desire to have it with one woman.

Normally, men use sex for fulfillment when we cheat. But by itself the sex isn't fulfilling, which is why we don't normally settle down with the women we've cheated with. In fact, nine times out of ten we will stay with the woman that is providing us with the other attributes such as loyalty, friendship and nurturing, and we'll seek the sex somewhere else. We need the sex, but we need the other pieces to complete the puzzle.

The way to keep us is to give us a Class A License to the Nookie Opportunity!

Believe me, a man that gets a balance of sex with the other attributes is far less likely to ever cheat or flee commitment. No matter what comes his way, he knows a good thing and finding a woman that is willing to be well-rounded in her approach to keeping the relationship going is most definitely a good thing.

How to Spot a Cheater

The easiest way to keep from being cheated on is to not get involved with a cheater in the first place. Some people may think you can never really tell if someone is or isn't a cheater, and that's true. There is no stereotypical look or person that you can expect to cheat. But often enough people ignore the obvious signs that would have kept them out of harm's way.

Take it from me, most cheaters show their stripes early. Of course there are exceptions, but if you learn to ask the right questions and look for the signs, you can spot potential cheaters early.

Here are a few basic skills to help spot a cheater:

ASK THE RIGHT QUESTIONS

Cheaters prey on the ignorant. When a woman asks the right strategic questions, a cheater will shy away from them. They get annoyed and it feels like it may take too much work to keep up the charade.

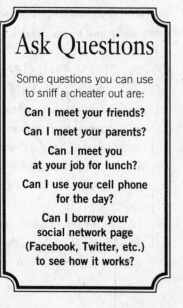

Ask Questions

Some questions you can use to sniff a cheater out are:

Can I meet your friends?

Can I meet your parents?

Can I meet you at your job for lunch?

Can I use your cell phone for the day?

Can I borrow your social network page (Facebook, Twitter, etc.) to see how it works?

You should also be willing to offer the same access to them in return. If you find that all of the answers to your questions are no, or you're being asked why you need these things, then the odds are there is something to be concerned about.

REQUEST THEIR AVAILABILITY

Cheaters aren't readily available because obviously they're dividing their time up behind the scenes. Asking a cheater for their availability and expecting that they will make themselves available for you is a surefire way to figure out if you're being played.

If someone never has time for you; asks to see you at weird hours or can't make themselves available per your requests, then obviously something's up.

GET THEM TO PROVE THAT THEY ARE SINGLE

In this day and age, you can't accept that someone is single because they say they are. Asking them to show you where they live or having them pick you up in their car are two ways to see their environment to decipher if anything seems out of the ordinary.

Someone who makes excuses why they can't take you to their house either lives with their mother, or has something to hide. Either way, it's probably better to keep it moving.

OFFER THEM THE OPPORTUNITY
TO GET INVOLVED IN YOUR CIRCLE

One of the things that a cheater likes to do is hide in the dark. Not only do they want to keep you away from their friends or inner circle, but they don't want to take chances that they will be spotted by someone in yours.

Asking them to meet your friends, family, associates or anyone else that you trust to give you an honest opinion may pull a cheater out of their comfort zone. It's normal for someone interested in a woman to want to see her environment, so if he doesn't, then that should be enough of a sign to not take the chance. If he does, the wisdom you receive from your circle may help to ease your mind if you are misjudging someone at all.

GO OUT LOCALLY

A cheater usually takes their real woman out locally, and takes the others outside of their immediate area or keeps things on the low by only going to their house or a hotel.

Asking them to take you to local restaurants, clubs, movie theaters, museums, malls and any place where they hang out regularly, is one of the best ways to find out who you're dealing with.

Keep in mind that if a guy is willing to take you to his local spots and put you within his environment, then he's either a really good cheater, or a really good guy.

Five Signs
a Man is Cheating

If you were being cheated on, would you recognize the signs? Some signs may be obvious but some you might not expect are actually right in front of your face. Notice the signs and you may save yourself time and energy from dealing with a heartbreak.

Here are the top five signs that cheaters use to get over:

Hides or keeps secret phone calls, emails, passwords, text messages

Spends secret or private time on computer or social network page

Doesn't involve you with his friends or inner circle

Has condoms but doesn't use them with you

Has secret stash of sex enhancement pills

Finding Out if a Man Can Be Faithful

When men and women first start to date, we will usually traditionally go through a ritual of Q&A's that, for some reason, makes us all feel comfortable with each other. It's instinctual to a degree, and we all do it naturally.

The beginning of any relationship is generally the time when a woman deciphers if she feels that a man is a viable candidate for something long-term or simply a quickie. If she's interested, she'll ask him a few questions to help her get to know who he is, or at least she thinks.

The basic questions will generally go something like this:

- Where are you from?
- What's it like there?
- Do you have any brothers or sisters?
- Are you close to your family?
- What's your relationship like with your mother?
- What kind of music do you like?
- What do you do for a living?
- What kind of car do you drive?
- Do you like kids?
- What do you do for fun?

The questions may vary from person to person but you get the gist. While these questions are fine to open up the dialogue, none of them actually clue a woman in on who a man truly is, at least not if she wants to know if he'll be able to be faithful or not. In fact, these questions can often be distractions from a woman getting the most important piece of information that she'd need in order to make an intelligent decision on a man.

What good does it do to have a man that drives a nice car or has a good relationship with his mother if he can't be faithful to a woman, right?

If a woman really wants to find out if a man can be faithful, they have to learn to ask this real and necessary question. Then they can forgo most of the elementary and frivolous questions and get to the bottom line that concerns all relationships.

What every woman should be asking a man is, "Have you learned how not to cheat?"

Based on a man's answer and in some cases, even the way that a man answers this question, a woman can find the information she'll need to know if a man can be faithful or not.

You see, if a man responds with a question or tries to find out what she means, he is probably not fully conscious of his innate cheating nature, or he is shocked that a woman would be conscious enough about a man's nature to ask about his cheating.

Cheaters usually have a hard time discussing the subject, and they may not be able to be real with themselves yet, or may even have something to hide.

However, if a man answers definitively yes or no, he is conscious of his manhood and is probably a critical thinker who cares about the consequences of his actions. This would also probably be reflected in other areas of his life, and although it does not ensure that he is the right man for her, it definitely means that he is a real candidate.

So, ladies, the next time you find yourself interested in a man, go ahead and get comfortable, but don't waste time on the small things. When the moment is right, pop the real question: "Have you learned how not to cheat?"

How to Keep a Faithful Man Committed

Popular thinking amongst women is that there are circumstantial reasons that men cheat. This seems rational to them because most women cheat as a reaction to the circumstances they are in with cheating men. But for men, cheating isn't circumstantial like it is for women, but staying committed is. Even men who don't have a problem being faithful say that it isn't always easy to stay committed. And no matter how faithful a man is, staying committed to one woman is a difficult task for even the most dedicated monogamist.

Before we go any further, let me point out that staying faithful doesn't necessarily mean staying committed, nor are they mutually exclusive. So let's define the two of them.

THE DIFFERENCE BETWEEN BEING COMMITTED AND BEING FAITHFUL

If you've ever been in a relationship, you may have noticed that for many people, there is a difference between being faithful and being committed. We have been taught for so long that they are one in the same, but they are not. Not knowing the difference can make it hard to avoid mistaking someone's issue with commitment, as being a problem with being faithful.

"Being Faithful" means to keep the agreement that governs your intimate relationships with other people inside of a committed relationship. As long as two people in a relationship stay true to their agreement, and that goes for any agreement they want, they are being faithful.

"Being committed" is a little more intricate because it is not based on an agreement of a set of rules on how or what you do in a relationship. Being committed more so means to stay dedicated to the relationship itself.

Being or staying committed often requires us to re-dedicate ourselves to our relationships on a perpetual basis. It may also mean that both people have to stay dedicated to working on keeping the relationship fresh in order to make a lasting shift from individual independence to jointed commitment. This has always proven to be a little bit more difficult for men than women; mostly because men are bred to conquer and women are bred to nurture. And as we all know, nurturing helps to build longevity; conquering does the opposite.

These very different gender-specific attributes make it hard for men and women to understand exactly how to keep a partner committed to the relationship. And because women haven't yet learned to read the signs when men are losing our commitment to a relationship, they often think we are having problems with being faithful, when it's a rededication that is needed.

WHEN A MAN NEEDS TO CONQUER

Lots of women make the mistake in believing that a faithful man no longer needs to conquer. Women often associate our conquering with cheating and in their minds, when a man isn't cheating, he no longer desires to be a conqueror.

This can be a big mistake because the truth is, most men that don't cheat need to conquer even more. When we've learned how to deal with the urge to conquer women, we need to replace it with conquering other things. We show it by constantly tackling new tasks in business, sports, video games, hobbies and even coaching our children in multiple activities.

You see it in a lot of married men that don't cheat. They start to do things to take their attention away from the commitment to the relationship. Taking on tasks with a new and aggressive vigor, a man might all of a sudden want to build things in the garage and backyard, rebuild cars, take on a house upgrade or tackle coaching their kid's youth sports team and act like they are competing for the world championship.

Men need to conquer and if the conqueror side of a man isn't nurtured, he will eventually flee commitment.

When women see this happening, their first response is to try and nurture the man back into the relationship. But that rarely works. While it may feel more natural for a woman to try to nurture a man's feminine side, we men don't normally even want to admit that we have a feminine side; leave off have it nurtured. The trick is to allow us to feel like conquerors in the daily little things to help us to stay committed in the long run.

WHAT IS CONQUERING?

Conquering for a man used to mean to be in control of women. Back in the day, the conquering man was looked at differently and it was quite normal that a man was controlling with a woman.

But those days are over, as the independence of women doesn't allow for them to be controlled by anything or anyone. So, instead, men today aspire to conquer by leading. That is why a man takes on the tasks of rebuilding a car in the driveway or coaching his son's Little League football team to a championship; he wants to conquer something.

Let's set the record straight about conquering, once and for all. Men no longer feel superior to women. But we also don't want to feel like we are women. Equality for us doesn't mean that we should both have the same roles in the relationship, home or daily tasks. When a woman allows us to take the lead without challenging us, we feel manly and that helps us stay committed to the relationship.

Being able to have the small things that we see as "a man's role," without having a woman battle us for them, helps men to feel like conquerors again. It's fantastic that women have achieved their independence, but they must also be careful to keep in mind that men need to feel adequate.

HOW MEN CONQUER

Relationships are true investments; learning how a man conquers is an overlooked asset that every woman can use to help a man stay committed.

Again, in a relationship, a faithful man still feels the need to conquer something. If a woman's actions block that natural instinct, then she risks making the man feel inadequate. And that may cause a man to flee or try to conquer her, and neither of those reactions help to preserve a long-term commitment.

Some women may think that being equal means being the same and that way the playing field would be even. "Why do men have to try to conquer everything anyway?" I've heard them ask. But that's like asking why birds fly or the sky is up and not down. Some things simply are the way they are, and if we can accept them, we can move ahead.

Men don't care if women know the keys to our behavior—as long as they allows us to feel like we are conquerors, then we're fine.

A great way to get started is by learning the characteristics of a man's conqueror side. Here are a few questions to help you analyze your faithful man:

- **When does he try to conquer?**
  (feel threatened, want control, to get his way, etc.)
- **What are the signs that he needs to conquer?** (he attacks, withdraws, etc.)
- **How does he act when he's conquering?**
  (aggressive, demanding, indifferent, etc.)
- **What actions does he take to conquer?** (takes charge, pushy, leads, etc.)

HOW TO HELP HIM FEEL LIKE A CONQUEROR

Helping a man feel like a conqueror will help him want to stay committed. It may sound odd to women, but it can be easier than you may think.

Why do men love a "ride-or-die woman"? "She doesn't get in the way," one of my buddies told me about his wife. It's true; she allows him to do the things that cause him to feel like a conqueror and that helps him to feel like she's going to ride with him no matter what. When a man feels that he has this type of woman, he will go the extra mile to stay committed because he sees her as an asset to his life. And ladies, keep in mind that just because you are in a relationship, doesn't mean that you're an asset...many women become liabilities.

Men love to feel like a woman will do something out of her comfort zone for us. In other words, she'll ride, no matter what. It's all about the little things that help us keep our heads in the commitment.

For instance, a man wants to take on a task that you see is menial. If a woman makes him fight or justify it, then she may cause him to flee. Allowing him to do it without hassle, and trusting that he is a faithful man who simply needs to conquer something, will make all the difference in the world.

I'm not suggesting that women should give men whatever they want all the time, but it's important for women to know that a man doesn't always want what he's asking for; he wants to know that his woman will ride with him if he asks. That makes him feel like a conqueror and that he has a ride-or-die type of woman.

It's really that simple…the small things make a man feel like a king!

Little do most women know that a small task like pushing the elevator button can be important to a man. We have all been in the elevator when a little boy gets in and wants to push the elevator button and his mom lets him do it. What seems like such a menial thing to a woman can be a task of conquering for a man.

I used to have a girlfriend that battled me on simple issues like where we parked when we went somewhere. No matter where I wanted to park, she'd argue that we should park somewhere else. To her she had just as much right to pick the parking place as I did.

While she was in the right to voice her opinion about the parking decision, battling me over an issue where I needed to feel like a conqueror only served to cause me to try harder to conquer. So we'd argue back and forth and I'd park where I wanted to just to conquer, or I'd reluctantly give in and flee. For a while I pleaded my case to her and tried to get her to understand that little things were important to me as a man. But she decided that it was more important to her that we were equal in all decisions and in the long run, our relationship was lost in her conquest.

However, my next girlfriend saw that this was important to me, so instead, she placed her concerns on making sure that we were always on time and as long as we were safe, she allowed me to choose the parking without hassle.

Again, it may sound like no big deal to a woman, but making that small decision helped me to feel like I had conquered, and in return, I made sure I accommodated her desire to always be on time.

Those little nuances serve to remind a man how valuable a woman is in the moments where he may tire of commitment.

On a larger scale, the thing that most faithful men complain about is that they can't get sex when they want it in a committed relationship. When a man is single or cheating, he can have sex at random or whenever he wants it. But when he's in a committed relationship, his sexual fulfillment is based 100 percent on the clock of his woman.

As I said earlier what many women may not see is that for a faithful man, being committed to a relationship gives us a sense of entitlement to sex. If we can't have it at our leisure, we feel rejected and no conqueror thinks he should ever be rejected. If it persists, we won't cheat, but it can cause us to pull away from the commitment.

Ladies, I understand that men always want sex and that can be inconvenient for a woman. Some women complain that they love having sex with their man, but they can't keep up with giving it the way a man needs it—all the time.

When a woman shows frustration, she can cause a man to feel that he isn't welcome to have what he believes is his. Because he can't take the cave man approach and drag her into his cave, he may retreat in frustration. This causes a lot of men to pull away over time and want to get out of the commitment where he is faced with such restriction.

Instead of completely turning him away, another approach is for a woman to negotiate without him knowing. Let him know that if he's willing to wait until the more convenient time, he can have it the way he likes it. This helps him feel like he can have it if he wants, but that she will fulfill his larger desire if he nurtures her needs as well.

As women find themselves at these little crossroads every day in relationships with faithful men, they can keep us engaged in commitment by allowing us the small things that make us feel like conquerors. Remember, just because a guy doesn't cheat, doesn't mean he doesn't still have all the desires of a conquering man.

If you help your man feel like a conqueror, then he'll be less likely to stray and look for other places or things to conquer. So don't underestimate the power of the small things. Remember that if it seems small to you, it's probably big to him.

How to Become First in a Man's Life

I t's no secret that throughout history man has been considered the head of the family. That has pretty much widely been considered the natural order of things and to most men, that meant that we came first in all things and literally controlled the family as a whole.

But today the thought of a woman putting a man first has become out of date and is even considered chauvinistic by many women.

What is it about a woman putting a man first that makes modern women cringe?

Could it be that too many good women have put badly trained men first and gotten burned?

Everyone knows that bad news travels fast, and over hundreds of years, the global domination of male cheating has reached the farthest corners of the globe and women of all types of ethnicities and faiths have either been burned by it or heard all about it.

Each time a man cheats and a woman gets burned, another layer gets added to the wall of protection that has been built in the female communal mind. That has caused them to abandon the once adored concept of putting a man first or placing him at the head of the relationship. Instead they have taken up arms against us; literally in some cases.

For women, that wall may have seemed like it would protect them from being taken advantage of by cheating men, but it made the problem worse. The average guy feels entitled to come first in a relationship. If he feels he's not being put first or has to fight for that spot, he feels unappreciated and powerless.

And although women today go to work like men do and communally feel that they should also be able to be put first in their relationships and families, men are not built to accommodate that. Whenever we see men that do accept it, we find them meek, unhappy and unfulfilled.

So this forces us to ask the question: In this day and time, who should come first? After all, both people can't come first; can they?

Yes, they can and they should. And to address this issue, men must show women that they can in fact come first, by putting us first. In a roundabout way, that also means that women choose to come second, which makes them first.

Make sense? Let me explain…

WHY SECOND ISN'T GOOD ENOUGH

First, men must accept that because we took advantage of our leadership positions and cheated on women, we have to man-up and prove ourselves. We also have to understand that some women will not want to immediately see the value in putting a man first until we've shown them how this, in fact, will make them first.

It can only work successfully when a man responds to a woman's virtuous generosity by putting the woman first in exchange. Any man that chooses to use a woman's generosity for power over her is insecure and not worth being with anyway!

At the same time, women need to also understand that to a man, there is a world of difference between first and second. And this difference governs everything that a man does in life. You can't have a harmonious relationship if the man feels second. It's not a right or wrong thing, ladies; it's how we are wired.

The perfect example is sports. Ask a man "who came in second" in their favorite sports championship last season and you'll be hard pressed to find one that can remember. We only remember the team that came in first; or another way to see this is we don't see that a team or athlete finished second; we see it as they lost.

But ask a man "who lost" the fight or the championship and it's easier for him to remember them because he attaches them to who beat them—the winner, or in this case, the one who came in first.

In real life, relationships aren't a competition. But when it comes to a man feeling like he's not being put first, the competitive nature comes out of us. Simultaneously, when we feel like we are being put second in our relationships or families, we feel that we've lost and again, a man needs to feel like he's the winner.

Acceptance of this is key for women, because as much as a man can change and evolve, women can't expect that men will be able to change their natural male instincts. However, we should not let our instincts rule us.

Growing as a man also means getting past some of the ideals that shaped earlier concepts of men, but it's imperative that both men and women understand the difference between an ideal and a fact. Ideally speaking, we are equal and should be treated equal in relationships, but the fact is men aren't wired to come in second, but they can learn to put women first.

HOW TO BECOME FIRST IN A MAN'S LIFE

When a woman puts a good man first, he feels empowered. That empowerment helps him feel like he's in the driver's seat and he will want to drive. In urban terms, that kind of woman is called a "ride-or-die chick." She is literally down to ride with her man for better or worse.

Ladies, before you choose to ride or die with a man, you should first know that he is capable of handling the responsibility. That doesn't necessarily or exclusively mean in financial terms. It also includes his level of maturity, wisdom and discipline.

Men should be tested during the dating process to demonstrate that they can make mutually beneficial decisions for the both of you. If a man isn't doing that, he's not a good candidate for a ride-or-die woman.

But once a man proves that he is capable of handling the power that a woman gives him, she must allow him to steer. Again, a good man will want to utilize his power to empower others. And empowering his woman comes first and foremost. He will show this by living a lifestyle that places her first in all things and makes her feel secure.

He will also consider the consequences of how his decisions affect her in his daily walk and his lifestyle will be an exercise in putting her first.

And there you have it—by a woman putting a good man first, she becomes first.

Pockets Over Pedigree

Women today are what I like to refer to as "Cheating Man Prone"... that is to say that they are now more prone to meet and get involved with a cheating man because of the way they evaluate men as candidates for relationships. One of the main reasons why today's women often find themselves involved with cheating men is because they look for "Pockets Over Pedigree."

"Pockets Over Pedigree," or "POP," means that women place their emphasis on how much a man makes, over how a man is made.

There is no secret that today's women are capable of achieving their own financial security. In return, they demand a man that can do the same. That isn't as easy as it has been in years past as issues of economics have caused a steep decline in a man's ability to have steady employment and produce an income that is substantial enough to support a wife and family on his own. Consequently, women have had to step up their game and make their own money.

Historically though, most women were trained from birth that finding a husband with a suitable family name was a woman's most important task in life. If she did, she'd be able to have a family that was esteemed in society. That meant that from birth, women were trained to get a husband who was well-bred by his parents and extended family to continue the family name. And in complement to that role, a part of such a man's basic understanding was that a woman would expect him to take care of her. And that meant, even above him loving her forever, he would financially support her.

For years a man's "Pedigree" preceded his financial worth. His family name entered the room before he did and his worth was often determined by it, over and above his individual finances.

Looking back to the renaissance, a woman that had to work was looked down on, and any woman that couldn't acquire a man of desirable namesake was said to be worthless; even by her own family.

The same went for slaves where a male and female slave's value was judged based on the pedigree of their owner. While that is an extremely dehumanizing concept, it shows the power that a well-respected name carried with it.

It wasn't just that a man's name was the definition of his pedigree. Having a pedigreed name also meant that he was educated and groomed at the proper schools and or military academies, or that he was of hero stock—meaning his father was a respected military or law enforcement man.

My friend Mohammad from Uganda told me that when he and his brothers looked for wives, along with their education, they also looked at a woman based on what her father's position was during Idi Amin's reign. Because Mohammad's father had been a part of the movement that removed Amin from power, if a woman's father represented the opposite position, then, in their eyes, she was not of pedigree.

Once a mother's key responsibility was to raise her daughter to be an appealing candidate to a man of prominent family status. A woman who had such status was well-kept, as they said in old times, because she had the ability to stay at home and focus on building the family. Homemaking and nurturing children were her main focuses and she was never expected to learn a trade other than those, which society believed came natural to her anyway.

Women who were able to have that lifestyle achieved a certain social status in all circles and women who were less fortunate looked at women of pedigree as being pampered.

It wasn't until the women's liberation movements ushered in women that fought to be educated and to enter the work force alongside men, that women were able to help their husbands provide for their families. And not until the twenty-first century was a woman's ability to aid her man in the financial support of the family considered an asset, and with it, died the importance of building a pedigree.

Fast-forward to today and the ideal of marrying a man with pedigree has virtually disappeared from female society's consciousness as modern women have had to contribute to their family's financial support by any means necessary. Women now represent at least 50 percent of the annual household income and boast jobs as executives, entrepreneurs and the new "mompreneur." They have taken advantage of the equality with man, and the more they earn and contribute, the prouder and often more respected they are.

Let's face it, the days of the well-kept, stay-at-home wife and mom are virtually extinct. Many women that can afford to stay at home still run a home business to make themselves feel like they are contributing more than the traditional pursuits of their female ancestors.

Because men are no longer the sole breadwinners in the home, women no longer feel the need to have a man of pedigree. Instead, women now look to a man's pockets for security and affirmation that he is a good candidate for her future.

However, women fail to realize that money isn't indicative of training and simply because a man has money, doesn't mean he will have the training to make him capable of being a faithful or supportive husband and father. Having money only means that a man has the ability to earn a wage, but there are tons of examples where men with money have refused to spend it on taking care of a woman or a family. And that's why pedigree is important again.

For women to find men who have the necessary training to be good mates, women must look past pockets and shift their focus to what I call "The New Pedigree."

Even though pedigree is an old concept, the theory that a real man is bred is still true. But unlike the old days when pedigree was based solely on family name, the New Pedigree is shaped by social forms of background and training.

So, before any woman settles down with a man, she should get to know his pedigree and she can do so by examining the following.

WHAT IS THE NEW PEDIGREE?

EDUCATIONAL BACKGROUND

This comes first because most women are taught that if a man has achieved higher education, then he is a perfect candidate for a good job and that means relationship and family security. Although scholastic achievements do push responsibility on us, we can't assume that it teaches or prepares men for relationships.

Instead, a woman should look at the nuances that have shaped a man's social education first. Has he traveled? Does he have friends of different backgrounds? Was he involved in crime or has he been to jail? The last one is tricky because for some men this one could rule them out as candidates. So women must keep in mind that because someone may have had a run-in with the law doesn't mean they are of bad pedigree. If a man has been arrested, it's important to consider the cause, the age and the outcome. She may be surprised to find that he is a budding Nelson Mandela.

WORK EXPERIENCE

A rich man isn't always what he may seem. The question a woman should ask isn't does he have a job? But more like, can he keep a job?

The man that you meet may have a job at the time you meet him, but without knowing his history, you may not foresee that he might quit his job quickly because he lacks "stayability," or the ability to stick it out through the tough times. Remember, it's more important to get a man that will work smart than one that will work hard.

FRIENDSHIPS

My personal and professional motto is "I am only as great as the greatness with which I surround myself," and that includes my friends. Ladies, the guys that a man hangs out with will always represent his core values. If his friends don't work or are lazy, then a woman can expect that her potential mate will be the same; no matter how different she wants to believe that he is. Winners like to be around winners, so if his friends are losers, there it is.

It's equally as important to see if his friends are fly-by-night, or if he maintains a longtime trusted group. When a man has a trusted group of guys, it usually means they have enough history with him to be real with each other, and that's extremely important during your hard times with him, because a man turns to his friends when he is having trouble with a woman.

Another question is, do his friends endorse cheating by each other? I remember once when a friend of mine told my buddies and me that he'd cheated on his wife in Las Vegas with a stripper, he was let down by our disappointment in him. It turned out that once he didn't receive the group's endorsement for what he'd done, he felt crappy about it—not only the cheating, but also that he'd let down the group; peer pressure can be a hell of a ruler.

Sure, sometimes there is one guy in the wolf pack that is different, but the odds are that they are a pack because they have most things in common. So don't ever underestimate the friends; who they are tells the truest stories about a man.

PAST RELATIONSHIPS

Most women skip this part when getting to know a new man because they feel it's not about how the man treated other women; it's more about how he will treat them that counts. But those that forget the past are doomed to repeat it, I always say.

A woman should not be shy about asking questions about a man's prior relationships, nor should a man be shy about discussing them. Everyone has a past and there's nothing wrong with any of it, as long as it's been used to grow.

When people don't want to be transparent about their pasts, they usually have something to hide and that means trouble. But when someone has changed, evolved or grown from their pasts, they are excited to let you know so you can see how different they are.

Change means experience and there is truly no substitution for experience. It is a vital element to forming the new pedigree. If dealing with getting around someone's past is hard for you, look at your own past, and remember that it's better to be with someone who is experienced, than to become their experience.

HOW TO CHOOSE PEDIGREE

Lastly, the new pedigree isn't about using prejudices to shut anyone out; it's about finding the right mate for you as an individual. The old model of pedigree was prejudicial and disenfranchised anyone that didn't have a prominent family name or money to shape their qualifications.

The new pedigree should help each person shape a list of basic attributes that best pinpoint the background accoutrements that your potential mate should have. Because everyone has their own history, the goal is to find a person whose pedigree is suited to enhance the things that are truly important to building a future with you.

WHAT YOU CAN DO TO LEARN ABOUT SOMEONE'S PEDIGREE

Consider Their Pedigree

Here are a few more things to consider before you commit to any potential mate:

Mental / physical medical history

Have or take care of children

Marital background
(ever been married, divorced or engaged)

Role models / mentors
(core values)

Core values (top five)

Upbringing and social breeding
(with whom they spend most of their time)

Violent or abusive experiences

Achieved goals
(have they achieved and accomplished goals)

Ask them for the top five things that are most important to them

Set a time limit for you to get to know a potential mate: A reasonable amount of time is thirty days to learn about someone's basic pedigree, if you are speaking regularly over phone, social networks, emails, texts and traditional dating. Most men know within the first thirty days if they see you as wifey or not, so it doesn't take that long for them to show it.

Get to the real question: As you're getting to know someone, it's important to find out if a man is capable of monogamy. He should tell you up front what he's looking for; if not, then you shouldn't be afraid to ask the question that you need an answer to most of all: Have you learned how not to cheat?

The Valentine's Day Massacre

"Why are you doing this to me?" she questioned in desperation. "I thought we had something special. How can you leave me all by myself on Valentine's Day?" she said as she began to cry. That is a small piece to a story that I overheard between a guy that I knew while growing up and his girlfriend, Susan.

It was February 7th, exactly one week before Valentine's Day, and David was on the clock. He realized that it was time for his annual excuse to create some space between him and his girlfriend. "It's not like that, baby. I have to work and you know that. Don't worry, I'll make it up to you after Valentine's Day, I promise," he said, saving just enough of her spirits to keep her around.

What David knew was that one week from Valentine's Day was much too short a time for Susan, or any woman, for that matter, to get another man. Every guy is taken by then and that is the day that their women demand to be with them. What Susan didn't know was that David didn't really have to spend time traveling for work, as he'd claimed was the reason for not being able to spend time with her on the famous national day of love. Unbeknownst to her, she was the victim of an obvious scandal that her heart wouldn't allow her eyes to see.

David was actually a man with a wife and two daughters. His wife was a very loving woman that worked a 9-to-5 job and took care of his two baby girls with hopes to groom them for great men. Neither she nor her seven- and ten-year-old girls suspected that their father was a hard-core cheater with not only one, but two other women that he was "letting down easy," as he liked to call it, right before Valentine's Day.

I was fifteen years old and had really just begun to learn my way around relationships. David was a smooth-talking fireman with a muscular build that helped attract the ladies. Plus, his job took him away at odd hours, so in a way, it was the perfect set-up for his female exploits.

He'd decided to take my cousin KC and I under his wing to teach us everything we needed to know about breaking up with women around the holiday that most women adored. And we looked up to him for it.

By that time both my cousin and I had already been cheating, as had most, if not all of the guys around us. But specifically having to break up with girls around Valentine's Day was a new concept to us—mainly because until our mid-teens, the concept of having a girlfriend didn't involve sex or dating. You know how it is; you really only kiss and that's enough. But at fifteen and sixteen years old, we were beginning to face an entirely new female who wanted to have an exclusive date on V-Day to showcase that she had a man and was the special person in his life.

The conversation KC and I overheard was only one of many that Dave had over the years. In fact, it was one of two that he'd allowed us to listen to that evening. He was brief and concise, leaving her in tears, and him with the relief that he was free to be with his real woman—his wife—on Valentine's Day.

For KC and I, that moment was our graduation, if you will, from teenage players into full-fledged heartbreakers!

Fast-forward fifteen years later and I found myself doing just as David had taught me to do. It had never dawned on me that I was a part of playing the game of love and deceit. The only difference was that I didn't have a wife and two kids.

For years after David's lesson of sorts, I'd noticed that more men than I could have ever imagined were having these V-Day breakups all around me.

I learned that V-Day should have been thought of more like D-Day for millions of women because simply put, it is a day where millions of women are massacred. What I mean by massacred is that in one sweeping chop, their hearts are broken.

All throughout America, Valentine's Day is the day that most women find out the truth. They either are or aren't the love of their man's life. Truly, V-Day is a reckoning! The guy you've been dating dumps you within days of it or he makes some excuse that he can't spend it with you because of work or something. The truth is he knows he will have to spend time with his real woman on V-Day.

Then he gets you a little trinket or charm so he doesn't totally lose the nookie, but it's a buyout and women never expect it...or they don't want to deal with the truth that they've been played. So they hold on and enable the cheater to keep up the charade and that way they can save face.

Women everywhere find themselves in this position year after year. There is so much pressure for them to be a guy's Valentine, and those that are home alone on V-Day are thought of as poor souls with no one to love them.

The need to be attached to someone on V-Day is bred into us when we are kids. I remember my first V-Day. I was in elementary school and my mother bought me the little heart candies with colorful words on them. You know, the ones that say Love and Cute on them and spell out "would you be my valentine." I was just old enough to have a crush and my mom made sure I had the card and candies. But it didn't stop there, because my arts and crafts teacher had all the kids making Valentine's Day cards to give to each other. We were using glue and macaroni noodles to spell out "Valentines." How much more breeding does a child need before the day becomes a part of their consciousness?

From there it becomes second nature for women to need a box of chocolates or a necklace from a man as an expression of his love. If he doesn't do it, then in her mind, he doesn't really love her.

And that's how we get locked into the V-Day ritual. The only way out for cheating men is the Valentine's Day Massacre!

HOW TO TELL IF YOU ARE NOT THE ONE

You can lie to yourself and believe that the things in the box to the right don't apply to your particular situation, but if you've been putting in the time and he isn't with you on V-Day, then you are not the one—period!

Now let me clarify that some men do have to work on Valentine's Day. Police officers, UPS workers and yes, even firemen, may have to devote time on the j.o.b. during the day of amour. But for the most part, most men know it's coming and set up time so they can spend it with their love. We don't really have a choice; there are so many commercials and advertisements dedicated to ensuring that it is on our minds that it's almost impossible to miss it.

And even if a guy does really have to work or is away, he can make time to communicate with you online. It's nothing to video chat and let you know that he's not doing dirt and that you're the one. Trust me, guys in the military that are away from home have to do it all the time.

So point blank, if a man is not spending V-Day with you, either physically or online, then you know that you're not the one.

You're Not the One If...

Here's how you know if you're not the one and only a man has for V-Day:

Breaks up with you a week before V-Day

Breaks up with you on V-Day

Says he can't make it on V-Day

Sets up a weird time to be with you on V-Day

Wants to spend time with you before or after the V-Day

Doesn't get you anything— not a card, candy, flowers, or even a handwritten letter

His phone is turned off on V-Day.

He gets irregular phone calls, text messages or tweets on V-Day.

He gets new photos of other women on his phone.

His social network profile says "single" on V-Day.

THINGS A MAN DOES TO SHOW YOU'RE THE ONLY ONE ON V-DAY

Overall, if you're the one, then he'll want to spend time with you. If he's not, then again, you're not the one!

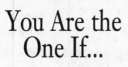

You Are the One If...

He can't afford the super-expensive prices that restaurants charge on V-Day, he may try to cook you a simple dinner at home.

He will surprise you at work for lunch.

He will send you flowers at work so your female co-workers see you've got a man.

He will take you for a quiet walk so it's only the two of you.

He will take you to the place of your first date.

He will offer to buy a bottle of your favorite wine or champagne.

He will Skype or iChat with you if he's out of town or has to work.

He will offer to give you a bubble bath and a massage at home.

He will propose.

THE TRUTH ABOUT VALENTINE'S DAY

Fundamentally speaking, Valentine's Day is not for men—it's for women. Most men know that it's a day to make our women feel special. We learn early on what's expected of us and go along with it to keep a happy relationship.

However, many women want men to be as excited about V-Day as they are. Somehow they see it as "our" day together. But ladies, don't expect that your man will always get excited about V-Day; it's not "our day" unless you make it so.

V-Day has lost some of its luster for men over the years because a lot of women demand that men spend great amounts of money on them; basically forcing them to prove their value by buying them gold or diamonds so they can impress their friends. That has caused many a guy to resent V-Day and pull away from the romance that it should represent.

Yes, a guy should spend time with his woman and show her that she is the one. But if his life is demanding of his time or money, making him buy expensive gifts or presents that he may not be able to afford, can be damaging to the relationship. I've definitely known my share of guys that get out of relationships with financially demanding women and immediately look for a woman that can share in the efforts.

With this in mind, women can help keep men interested in investing in the romance and time together on V-Day by contributing to the experience.

Guys also like to feel special on V-Day. Don't get it twisted; there isn't a man that wouldn't love to show his buddies his new Rolex that his woman bought him for Valentine's Day. But we don't expect it nor do we feel like we should ask for it. Making us feel special doesn't necessarily mean that we want anything in particular, but we are definitely more likely to invest in the romance of the day if we know that we will also receive something special from our woman.

WHAT WOMEN CAN DO TO KEEP FROM BEING DROPPED ON V-DAY

If a woman wants to ensure that she is the one on V-Day, she must let the man know that "she is the one." For guys, that means showing us that our women have a certain expectancy to be with us.

Why wait for us guys, ladies? Without being pushy a woman can put things in motion to ensure that she doesn't end up in the cold. The small suggestion that a woman is going to make plans will reveal if a guy intends to spend time with her or if he's got something else up his sleeve.

Remember, if you don't act like you are the one, why should he treat you like you are?

Remember, there are twenty-four hours in a day, so a man that has multiple women probably has good time management. It's very hard for a man to spend the night

Find Out If You're the One

Here are a few ways to get the ball rolling to find out if you're the one on the most romantic day of all.

Plan your own private time and let him know when to arrive.

Instead of asking him what he'd like to do, offer him suggestions of what can be done—both high-end and affordable.

Offer him the opportunity to have dinner with you or to have you for dinner.

Plan a V-Day party at home for him and your close friends.

Ask him what time he will be available after work and surprise him at his job before he gets off.

Tell him you're thinking about taking the day off and ask him if he can as well.

If you don't live together, ask him to spend the night.

or spend the day with a woman if he's got other women pulling at him for his time. If he's spending the day with you or sleeping over, then the odds are he's not juggling women on V-Day.

I've always prided myself in knowing my woman's essentials. Her shoe size to her bra size—it's all so I can get something for her at any given moment. A woman should also know her man's essentials, and V-Day is the perfect opportunity to learn them.

Ladies, Valentine's Day can be the exact excuse you needed to upgrade your man and make him feel special in the process. Here are a few examples of how you can personalize your V-Day and make your man feel special.

Model Your Sexy Underwear: Try out those new boy shorts, thongs and G-strings. Instead of doing the typical V-Day red, go for his favorite color.

Sport His Favorite Team Gear: Oh yeah! The super-short, skin-tight jersey of his favorite team will do the trick.

Rent His Favorite Car: Rent his favorite car to make the ride to and from dinner extra sexy.

Get Him a Watch: Every man should have a good watch; splurge on him within budget.

Get Him Shoes: Guys have to stay up on their shoe game as well, and women can lead the way.

Get Him a Suit: Get him something that you'd like to see him in all the time. Learn his correct suit size and put it on your tab. Then pull it out on V-Day as you get ready for dinner. He will feel like James Bond in *Casino Royale*.

Get a Tattoo: No, you don't have to get a real tattoo; opt for one of the temporary fake ones in his name. Plenty of shops do them now and you can get it put in his favorite personal spot on your body so he feels extra-special at the right moment.

Most importantly, when a woman shows her attraction to her man on V-Day it will cause him to want to keep the romance going. It's not about telling him how good he looks or smells…it's about showing your attraction in your actions. And ladies, nothing says you're attracted to us like a night of mutual appreciation, if you get what I'm saying!

The Truth About Freaks and Good Girls

"*She's a very kinky girl, the kind you don't take home to mother,*" Rick James said in his '80s hit song "Super Freak." Although it was decades ago, the girl Rick was describing is still considered a freak—some even called a super freak.

Let me clarify for those who may not know what a freak is.

"A freak is a female that provokes and indulges in extreme sexual activities." There are a few types of freaks, so let's name and define them here.

THE JUMP-OFF:

She thinks that she is wifey material but men only see her for one thing—sex. A lot of times she is surprised to learn that the man she's been having sex with only wants her for sex. But that's because she doesn't position herself to get anything more than sex from him.

FREAK OF THE WEEK:

Formerly known as the "one-night stand" or the "weekend girl." She is willing to get down and dirty for a short fun time and then move on. This type of woman is sometimes married or in a committed relationship and is in search of some outside excitement.

UNDERCOVER FREAK:

This female is a favorite for men because on the outside she doesn't look like a freak, but behind closed doors, she's buck wild. Internally, she denies that she is a freak, so she prefers to explore her sexual wild side without people knowing her personal business.

STRAIGHT FREAK:

This woman is straight up! The kind of female that tells a man she wants sex and isn't shy about the kind of sex she wants. In other words, she is straight up about what she wants and what she can do.

SUPER FREAK:

The type of woman that drives men crazy because she flaunts it and gives it. The super freak will go the extra mile in bed. She doesn't have any inhibitions when it comes to sex and is down anytime, anywhere and anyplace, because she doesn't care what people think.

There are also the women that may portray sex visually, because it makes them feel sexy, but they may not even have sex with you. The goal is to drive your mind wild with thoughts of sex, especially sex with her, even though you can't have her. We call her a play freak.

No matter how hard we men fight it, there is a freak for every type of man on earth and when we meet the one that's right for us, we can't resist her.

Freaks are tempting because men are taught that only good girls make good wives, and the perception of a freak doesn't fit the good-girl stereotype. But you don't hear that good girls make good nights. So when a man sees the kind of freak that he likes, it instantly makes him want her sexually. Her provocative persona is taboo for his thoughts of having monogamy and he can't help but want what she has to offer.

That's why it's important that every woman have a little freak in her. Most women do, but don't want to show it to men because they feel it makes men think they are promiscuous. Even after marriage, the average wife doesn't want her man to think of her that way. But ladies, that's where you go wrong! A man doesn't want to marry a freak because he doesn't believe she has the qualities of a good girl. But that doesn't mean he doesn't want a good girl to have the qualities of a freak. A woman who works on her freaky-side is a smart woman!

If you ask men why they cheat, their biggest excuse is that they get bored with "Serial Sex." Serial sex is sex with one partner all the time and as much as it may be hard for a woman to accept, the truth is that men weren't set up for that. Generally speaking, men need sexual variety even after we're capable of being monogamous. That's why the sexy nurse and cop uniform was created for Halloween. It's not just a costume; if most men had the chance, they would really have sex with the nurse that takes their temperature during their physical or the female cop that gives them a speeding ticket.

You see, a man's experience with sex changes when he meets a woman that looks at sex through the eyes of a man—a freak. It completely throws us off guard because we've been taught that women don't think of sex the way that men do. That's what gives a freak power over us.

With a freak, men begin to see sex as an encounter of mutual participation, not mutual consent. No man wants to have consensual sex; that term only sounds right in court. Ultimately, men want women to participate in sex on the same level as they do.

My friend Tim is the perfect example. He met a woman who expressed that she needed sex frequently. It turned out that she needed it more than he did. At first he was intimidated by that and felt that his manhood was threatened. When he shared this with me, I understood why he struggled with it; especially because he was raised very religious.

His training, as with most men, was that women were supposed to be more docile when it came to sex. And that caused him to struggle with feeling inferior to her sexual appetite. At the same time, he was intrigued by it and he couldn't get her off of his mind. See, like I said, every man has a freak that's perfect for him.

I encouraged him to let himself look at her as a way to grow a new perception of women...one that would see them as partners, not things to conquer.

He agreed, and once he opened his mind, he saw that her sexual appetite was a perk. And before long, those feelings of intimidation turned into a mutual respect for her. Fortunately, she was the right kind of freak for him, and two years later, they got married.

Keep in mind that I'm not saying that women should want sex as often as men; that would be asking too much. But if they understand their inner-freak and know how to use it, women can garner mutual respect in their relationships.

We live in a time where we don't have to be ashamed or embarrassed about sexuality.

The old model of the woman who is reserved about her sexuality is out. Every woman should embrace her freaky side and use her consequence mechanism to measure when it's appropriate to use it.

So good girls, it's time for you to "get your freak on" and you can rest assured that when you do, the right man will be singing Rick James' other song—"Give It to Me Baby"!

Pulling a Yoko Ono

If you've ever watched one of the guy-type movies like the *Ocean's* series, then you've probably heard them use funny and catchy names and phrases to describe the methods they use to get something they want, or someone to do what they need.

In the spirit of those films, I have come up with my own phrase that will help save women everywhere from a life of worrying about their man cheating. This method will also give women power to enhance their long-term commitments with men in relationships.

It goes like this: when a man needs space from the confines of commitment, or his actions show that he needs a sexual hiatus within a long-term relationship, "this may be time for a Yoko Ono."

I am sure you are wondering, Maxwell, what the heck is a Yoko Ono? Well, sit back for a moment and let me teach you how knowing when to pull a Yoko One may save your relationship.

We all know Yoko Ono. She was the woman said to have broken up the Beatles. In the minds of millions of Beatles fans and followers, she had power over her husband, John Lennon, that lured him away from the band. As a former music executive, I recognize all too well the anger that a loyal fan can have toward anything or anyone that may cause their favorite group or band to break up. And at the same time, as a reformed cheater turned dedicated monogamist, I know all too well the power a woman can have within the mind of a man.

The power that I speak of can be a double-edged sword for a savvy woman; used correctly, it can carve out a perfect place for her in a man's life, getting him to forsake any and all others. But it can also cut her out of his life if or when the man becomes overwhelmed by allowing one woman to insulate him so much.

So when Yoko noticed that Lennon was needing a break from her and their relationship, she made a decision that even shocked the world of anything goes rock 'n' roll. She brought in another woman. But not just a stranger; in a very calculated move, Yoko devised a plan to have Lennon and the couple's assistant, May Pang, hook up.

The story goes that during the summer of 1973, Pang was working on the recording of Lennon's *Mind Games* album. Lennon and Yoko were having relationship problems and had decided to separate, so to protect her relationship and ensure that John would not get engaged in a dangerous affair, Yoko suggested to Pang that she become Lennon's companion. Yoko recognized that she and Lennon had been arguing a lot and were growing apart, and she admittedly said that she feared that Lennon would start seeing other women. She remembered that once Lennon had said that he found Pang sexually attractive, so it seemed to be the perfect opportunity for her to control the situation.

But when Yoko approached Pang about the idea, Pang said that she could never be sexual with Lennon because he was her employer and he was married to Yoko. But the older and more determined Yoko ignored Pang's fears and told her not to worry; she would personally arrange everything.

And that's exactly what she did. In October 1973, Lennon left New York for Los Angeles and took Pang with him for what he called "The Lost Weekend." During that period, Yoko allowed Lennon the freedom to be with May Pang, sexually uninhibited, in hopes that it would free up his mind to work and give him the time to get his head back into their relationship.

It sounds a bit off the edge for most people, but look at the results. Lennon became inspired and wrote two albums, and when he went back to Yoko, they had a baby son shortly thereafter.

Now don't get me wrong. I understand that setting your husband up with another woman is a very dangerous proposition for many women. But look at it through Yoko's eyes: she knew that the odds were that Lennon was going to be with other women, no matter what. So she figured, hey, if I set it up, then I can monitor and control it to the extent that I don't lose my man. That way Lennon didn't cheat and Yoko kept some power.

Ladies, I'm not suggesting that you should go around allowing your man to be with other women. But women can control cheating a lot easier if they allow themselves to be honest about their men and their relationships.

In their case, Lennon and Yoko were on the fringe of a breakup, and if he'd gone outside of the relationship, which most men will do, then Yoko would have lost him forever. Her goal was to keep him committed to the relationship, and because she understood her man, she acted to secure the long-term care of their union.

She could have enabled him to cheat, as most women would do by accepting the downward spiral of the relationship. And she could have also elected to cheat herself to make the playing field even. Instead, she opted to see the bigger picture and it worked.

Ladies, sometimes a long relationship can become a bit too overbearing for a man. It doesn't mean he doesn't love you or want to be with you, but he may need a break to take time to re-dedicate himself to the commitment of the relationship. Instead of letting him run free into the jungle, forcing yourself to worry about him cheating, it may be best to pull a Yoko Ono.

You don't want him out there left alone to his own folly. Even if he knows how not to cheat, all humans need a bit of a change and if left vulnerable, you take the chance of him losing focus on the bigger picture, which must always be to preserve the health of the relationship for a long-term commitment.

BUT WHAT IF HE STRAYS BECAUSE I SET IT UP?

Worrying about a man cheating or straying is indeed a very real and understandable consideration. I can imagine that Yoko was concerned about Lennon leaving her for Pang. But it would have been much worse if she'd allowed another woman to come into Lennon's life at his own discretion. She wouldn't have known her or her intentions and that would have presented a much more serious threat than Pang. Yoko was always able to monitor Pang's and Lennon's moves. She kept tabs on him (them) and she made sure that Pang took care of Lennon's manly needs in her absence.

That's a hell of a lot better than pulling a Catherine Becker. In case you aren't familiar with her, Catherine Becker is the woman that drugged her husband during dinner, tied him up and then cut his penis off.

Ever faithful, the forty-eight-year-old femme fatale Becker said that her husband of years had been cheating on her and she'd had enough. Enough to say the least—it's more like she'd decided that he'd had enough!

When the police questioned her motives, Catherine stated that the couple had been fighting back and forth about her husband's cheating for some time. But Catherine couldn't get him to stop and saw that the relationship was going to come to an end after she'd invested years of dedicated commitment to their marriage.

Unlike Yoko Ono, Catherine couldn't get control of the situation to head off her husband's cheating. So one day she snapped and lost it! In a confused mental state from the mental abuse that cheating causes, she devised a plan to get her revenge and make sure that her husband would never be able to physically cheat on her or any other woman again.

Calmly, Catherine covertly set up a spiked late-afternoon dinner that was laced with a drug for her unsuspecting husband to put him into a deep sleep. And so he sat and ate, without a thought that his actions were about to seal his own fate.

It wasn't long after he'd eaten his food that he fell into a coma-like sleep. Catherine pulled him from the table and tied him up. Naked and fully exposed with a flaccid penis, she began to work on him. Her sharpest knife sliced through his penis flesh like one of those commercials that we see on television for the ultimate cutting knife—you know the one: "Call now and get the knife and these handy-dandy companion personal slicers; all a $300 dollar value—yours for one low payment of $9.99."

With revenge and justice tightly twined in her mind, she had cut through half of him when he woke up. Not fully having gathered all of his senses, his body was numb from the drugs that he'd digested. Unfortunately, not numb enough to keep from feeling his member being chopped through. That was enough to wake him up to figure out what was going on.

Screaming at the top of his lungs for her to stop, she made her way through the final slice as he begged her in terror to please stop. But there would be no absolution for him; it was done. He was penis-less!

I can't help but wonder if at some point in his mind, while he reached for every ounce of strength he had to keep from fainting and dying, that he considered "hey, maybe they can reconnect it—yea, they have great medical technology today and they'll be able to save me from what this crazy bitch has done." But that would have been a quickly passing hope for naught, because right before his own eyes, Catherine took the penis and tossed it into the kitchen sink and pushed it into the garbage disposal. No water to help it go down, she shoved it deeply into the disposal's teeth and turned the switch—gnawing it to shreds, leaving him in shock as he watched the penis that he'd used to have sex with so many women behind his wife's back become shredded beef.

Gathering herself, Catherine then picked up the phone and called the police. She didn't hide or run; instead, she gave the police an admission that sounded more like a statement of vindication. When the cops arrived and asked her why she'd done such a horrible and calculated thing, Catherine smiled and said, "Because he deserved it."

I can't help but wonder if Catherine had pulled a Yoko Ono, would she have been able to salvage her relationship and reel her man in before they both reached that fatal point of no return? We will never know for sure... and let me also add that the threat of a man's infidelity is not a reason to let him go and sleep around. If so, men everywhere will be pulling tricks on women and we can't have that. But in consideration of the complex road of relationships that has to be navigated for long-term commitment, women should be prepared to handle men more progressively in today's world. That is, if their goal is really to sustain the longevity of a man's commitment and keep their own sanity along the way.

To do that it may require thinking outside of the box, ladies. And as uncomfortable as it may make some women who think they'd rather leave than to stay in a relationship and tolerate their man having sex with another woman; or for those who think that if a man really loves them, then he wouldn't even desire to cheat or need to be with another woman for the rest of his life, this should be a strong consideration before you or your man go off of the deep end.

Ladies, the bottom line is that you should know that you do have options that can aid you if you understand your man's nature and watch for the signs that he may stray. Of course a man should respect and uphold the sanctity of his commitment to a woman and learn how not to cheat. But if a woman pays close attention to her man, and dedicates herself to maintaining her relationship, then she may be able to keep her man from cheating with a little help from Yoko Ono.

Speaking words of wisdom: Let it be.

What Men Really Want in a Woman

How does a woman keep a man from straying? That's the billion-dollar question that every woman wants answered. It's not easy to figure men out. Our minds go in a billion directions every second and most of the thoughts we have involve sex.

Some studies indicate that a man thinks about sex every seven seconds. Have you ever wondered if that number included men in committed relationships? And if it does, do they think about sex with their mates every seven seconds, or sex with someone else?

On top of that, we men aren't ever taught what to do about those sexual thoughts. I asked tons of men in preparation for this book if they'd ever been taught what to do with the thoughts that they encounter in those seconds of lustful thinking. None of them, and there were fifty to be exact, had a father or mentor that gave them any training on how to handle their thoughts.

So then, what's a man to do? Should he act on his thoughts or allow them to pass? And what exactly is expected of us anyway? Why do women think that once we commit to them, that those thoughts will somehow magically disappear? They won't and we have no idea how to make them go away. Trust me, ladies, there are a lot of men that wish they could; it would make things a lot easier to deal with monogamy.

We end up in so much trouble with women because of the unbridled thoughts that travel through our minds. The thought precedes the action... when a woman catches her man looking at another woman, he's already had a thought about her. His look is his body reacting to the signal from the brain that says, *hey, we're attracted to her.* So c'mon, there is no right or wrong when it comes to thinking; it's purely chemical.

We men don't see our thinking as right or wrong, but women are often the deciding gender for how we are allowed to pursue our thinking. And maybe if women understood the way that we think better, they'd be more accepting of our thoughts. That's always been difficult because we men aren't the best at communicating to women what we want.

Most of us don't even know what we want, so how can we communicate that to a woman? It's impossible.

Plus, ladies, we're afraid of the consequences if we do. Let's keep it all on front street here...women haven't been very accepting of men who are honest with them about their inner-desires. Seven out of ten men say that they would never tell their women everything because they don't believe their women could handle it, a recent poll of men in America shows.

How can women expect men to tell them the truth if every time that we do, they judge it as right or wrong; or use it to make us think that we are somehow sexual deviants?

It's time we get to the truth!

WHAT YOU DON'T KNOW MAY HURT YOU

Ladies, you can keep living in the land of make-believe that you will get the one man that won't cheat on you, or you can come out of the matrix and accept us for what we truly are.

No, we're not dogs! We're afraid to tell you what we really want because we know you haven't been able to handle it. So if we're going to be progressive with each other, then let's start right here with the biggest truth of all.

Women can't handle their men desiring other women. You can't take him looking at another woman or her body parts. Men have tried to explain that it's not personal; we look at all beautiful things the same, but that doesn't work for women—you want exclusivity.

Then when you've finally reached the point of frustration because we won't budge on changing our nature, you pull the "let's make it even" card out on us. You know you do— "Well, let's make it even; if you can look, then so can I," you say. But that's revenge on men just for being our natural selves.

Let's try to take another look at this problem. It's not that men want to look at other women; it's that they have no choice. Try not to see this the way you operate or function; we aren't you…we are wired to look for things to hunt. Now, true enough, we shouldn't be hunting other women if we're in a relationship, but our instinct to look for food is still there. Get it?

If not, let me use myself as the example. Once I learned how not to cheat, I stopped looking for women to conquer. When I say "I," I'm referring to me the "Thinking Man" Maxwell Billieon. However, my nature or manhood still alerts me that there are things that it finds attractive around. But my conscious mind is able to direct it toward other things, deciphering what I should and what I shouldn't conquer.

So, you see, even when we don't cheat and are committed, our nature will always want to look. What a woman can do to control that is to learn to look with us. I didn't say learn to like it with us, but don't hate. There's nothing wrong with a woman seeing beauty with her man. It makes him feel like she's a friend and that he can be open and honest with her about the most taboo thing there is—the opposite sex. No, trying to make it even or fair so that you can look won't make him okay with it. The odds are he'll resent you for trying to compete and pull back, and that causes us to flee commitment.

Allowing a man to enjoy beauty, within reason, also makes a woman appear strong and above petty things. If he does it respectfully and doesn't hide it, then he can be trusted. Men love a woman that is secure in herself; especially when she knows that admiring beauty doesn't mean he doesn't love her beauty even more. It means that he's a man and trust me: if a man ain't looking with you, he's looking without you.

If you really want to get power with a man, become a woman that brings beauty to his attention. If you know that he likes boobs, when you see some that you know he'd peek at, don't be jealous…give him a tap to alert him. The same as you'd do with a pair of shoes or a shirt. Don't be afraid; if he's a good man, then he won't take advantage and use it as a license to go further.

If he does, then it was only a matter of time before he did anyway, so you did yourself a favor by finding out sooner than later.

WHY MEN REALLY GET MARRIED

When a man decides to get serious, he usually does it for love, or so he tells himself. But a recent poll of divorced men shows that there are other variables behind the ultimate decision for men and ladies, and they aren't what you think. The truth is, most men get married because they believe:

- It's the moral and right thing to do.
- It's expected of them.
- It's necessary to have children.
- It's best to carry on the family name.
- Their mate will make a good mother.

Is it just me or does this sound like men are getting married for all the wrong reasons to have happiness? It's no wonder that we immediately feel confined and trapped after we say, "I do." Never fear, ladies; these results don't necessarily mean that you are the blame. But it does show that what men are truly looking for is not so easily found.

To bring this home for me, I did my own poll and asked five men between the ages of thirty and forty-five what attributes they thought would make them want to be faithful to one woman for the rest of their lives. Here's what they said:

- She is capable of being my best friend.
- I respect her.
- She will be loyal no matter what comes.

That's it—they all seemed to want the same things; a woman that could be a loyal and respected friend. Sounds simple enough to me that if ladies have those qualities, then they should have no problem getting the man that they want, right?

So why aren't the masses of men finding these qualities when they look for women? Perhaps women don't have the correct information directly from the source. As a realist I'd like to keep it real, ladies. And I want to make sure you know what men are saying so that you can make well-informed decisions on how to handle your relationships.

Obviously, not all men are the same…but there are certain things that most men seem to want no matter what their background is. The following chapter will give you the basic insight into those things and if you use them, I guarantee that they will prove to help you keep your man from straying, or at least show you that you are with a man that isn't capable of being the man you need.

WHAT BAD GIRLS KNOW ABOUT MEN THAT GOOD GIRLS DON'T

Every man loves a bad girl! No, most men won't marry a bad girl but trust me, it's definitely not because we don't like them. It's more because we don't trust that they can also be good girls. I guarantee you that if a man could trust a bad girl, then he would marry her.

But men don't allow themselves to fall in love with bad girls. That's the reason why bad girls such as strippers and other women in similar fields have a harder time getting men to take them serious. I'm not saying they are bad people, but to men they are risky. After all, they don't have a shortage of interested men, but guys tend to only be interested in the bad girl side of them.

If they are so dangerous, then what is it that we men love so much about bad girls? Bad girls know how to have fun! Men know that they aren't restricted by traditional thought and for us, it's always fun to be with a bad girl because they keep us on our toes. They are a whirlwind of fun and sexuality…the perfect combination to pique a man's dopamine.

There are two types of fun for men: There's the kind that good girls like to have; and there's the kind that bad girls get to have with men. Every good girl should learn how to have that kind of bad girl fun.

For instance, bad girls aren't afraid to do guy things. They know that the more entrance they get into a man's world, the more they get into his head. It doesn't matter when, where or why; they are ready for it all.

A wise older woman that had been married for forty years once told me that every woman should accompany her man to a sports game, casino or even a strip club at least once. When I asked why a strip club, she said, "Because that's where bad girls work."

When a woman does this with a man, it works two fold for her: She learns the things that he likes that she may not have known, simply by watching his response to other women. And she can pick up a tip or two about what other women do to entice men. "What many women don't realize is that strippers don't just work the pole—they work the room. That's how they learn what every man likes," she added.

That's what bad girls do best; they pay attention to what men like and give it to them; not necessarily submissively, but with complete control.

They know what to wear, how to smell, walk, talk and communicate with their eyes to ensure that men desire them. And it doesn't stop there because once a bad girl gets a man's attention, she knows how to close the deal.

A bad girl is great at paying a man special attention to make him feel like he's the only man in the room. That's every bad girl's forte. They know that they can have any man if he thinks that he is "The Man." Good girls say they don't want to do that because it's an act and they feel like they are playing games and can't be taken seriously.

But it's not an act when you're in a relationship because the intentions are best for both people. By using this bad girl principle, any woman can easily make a man feel special enough to get what she wants and needs from him, and that's to stay committed and faithful.

A balanced man wants a woman to have that side to her, just like he knows that a woman wants him to have both a bad boy and a good guy side. He admires those sexy and liberating attributes in a woman and he respects her for knowing the rules of the game.

Remember, no one is perfect. We all have something we can learn from someone who is totally different than us. If a woman's goal is to learn what men really want, then she must perfect her ability to keep a man's attention. And bad girls have that part down pat.

WHAT GOOD GIRLS KNOW ABOUT MEN
THAT BAD GIRLS DON'T

Bad girls know how to have fun, and good girls know how to have one—one man that is. When it comes to giving a man what he wants, there is no substitution for loyalty. It is the no. 1 desired attribute in a woman on every man's list and it can be the glue that holds together relationships that have come apart in other areas. And plainly speaking, no woman should expect a man to stay faithful or committed if he can't trust that she is also 100 percent loyal.

Without a loyal woman, a man can't truly have peace of mind. His head becomes perpetually consumed by thoughts of his woman's possible infidelity when he should be focused on building the relationship. And no peace means no success!

As much as we like to have fun with them, guys believe that bad girls aren't the loyal type, so we watch our backs with them. Men will tell each other that they should be careful of a woman if she appears to be a bad girl. They are worried that in a relationship a bad girl is always working the room and available for someone who may have more money, fame or power than them. If a woman wants to have a committed relationship, then she has to be careful not to be thought of as a bad girl.

The fear of having a disloyal woman makes a man crazy; as much as he can't prove it, he knows in his mind when he has a woman that is only about having fun, and there's always more fun for her to find. For protection, he gets himself ready for any proof, so he can quickly exit the relationship. And any woman knows that when a man is looking for the exit, he will easily stray.

However, a good girl wants her man to commit and therefore, she shows that she is loyal to no limit. She's the kind of female that will turn her back on her friends and family if they don't like her man, even if they are right about him. No matter what the man does, he can do no wrong in her eyes and for a good man, that gift is invaluable. Oh yes, she is wifey material!

That's what men love about good girls so much; we know that they are loyal to their relationships and their men. Bad girls have what it takes to get us, and good girls have what we need to keep us committed.

With the right combination of both, a man is much more likely to be faithful and stay committed.

THE FIVE VIRTUES OF A WOMAN
EVERY MAN WANTS

Believe me, most men I interviewed are saying they want the same basic things. If women can truly learn these virtues, it will enhance their relationships. Here they are.

FRIENDSHIP

A man wants to be able to tell his woman anything without judgment. We desire to share our manhood with women as friends. When a man gets a woman who is his friend, he gets a companion. In turn he wants to share his life with her and everything that comes with it.

That ability to share without judgment naturally breeds trust in a man. Like with our buddies, we trust the guys that we can share the most with. When sharing with a woman fills that space, a man lets down his guard in other areas with ease.

If women want men to stay faithful and committed to them, they must learn to act as a friend without judgment. Create a space with a man where he can talk to you about his real desires. Ask him how he feels about taboo things and when he does, don't judge him. Instead, share your opinion about the thing; not what he thinks about the thing.

Men often find that when a woman does allow them to speak without judgment, she will form an opinion about what he thinks, instead of sharing her opinion on the issue, like friends do. Remember, getting him to share to see what he says so you can judge him is playing dirty pool and that will cause him to flee the commitment, I guarantee.

Work on taking a true interest in allowing him to make you his friend. You don't have to understand how or why he feels a certain way; accept that he does as a man.

ACCEPTANCE

Why is it bad to feel the way I feel? Men always ask this question...we don't understand why women demonize us for thinking differently than they do. We really can't help what we think, so we shouldn't be penalized for it!

Really, ladies, it's time to back off! No man is going to want to get close enough to be honest with you if he's not accepted when he does. By judging what men are or aren't supposed to think and want, you cause us to feel guilty for our natural desires and thoughts…and that's a huge reason that men say they flee commitment: they can't be free to be men.

Many of us stay in those relationships because we've convinced ourselves that all women are the same. So instead of looking for someone else, we stay and hide the truth. Women can sense when men aren't being completely transparent, but haven't yet made the necessary adjustments to get us to open up.

LOYALTY

I'm not sure where women got the idea that they should be able to understand everything that men want in order to do it. That's not loyalty—at least not to a man. Some women spread the word that men are supposed to justify our thinking to women to get them to accommodate our requests. Whoever told you this, ladies, she lied to you.

Men don't work like that. We know going into any arrangement where we are expected to be loyal, that we don't have to understand what we're being asked to do; we just do it because we've vowed to be loyal.

Our sports and military thrive on men's ability to do what they are told without questioning why. Women, on the other hand, always want to know why, how, when and who said so before they will commit to doing something that comes from a man's mind. To a man that's not loyalty and all the discussion and questions take way too much time away from getting the task done.

As I've said before, men love a ride-or-die type of woman. She knows when to ask questions and when to simply ride. If more women tried this approach, they would find that their men would be more open to explaining themselves when it counts. But the constant barrage of questions when we want or need something from a woman sounds like Charlie Brown's mother to us. Wah, wah-wah-wah, wah-wha-wha-wha!

Ladies, learning to trust that we've done our research and know how to get you from A to B is an asset for keeping a man. When a good man feels that you are loyal to him, he will make sure that he doesn't let you down by taking every advanced and precautionary step to consider the consequences. Once he's done that, he needs you to roll with him—be loyal.

Remember, men are conquerors and that part of us wants our women to support us and ride out. And that also means our women.

FEMININITY

There was once a time when women took pride in staying far away from anything that made them resemble a man. Our clothing, hair, speech and attributes that were masculine were off-limits to women and they reveled in their own femininity.

In the movie *Scent of a Woman*, Al Pacino plays a blind military officer that can tell a woman by her smell. That woman was proud to enter a room and not be seen as one of the boys. It gave her an edge over the male-dominated culture. However, women have had to assimilate into the corporate sexist world and that has caused a sort of "defeminization" of certain female traits.

Now a woman will show up to a dinner date wearing pants instead of a skirt or dress. Those pants will show off her curves, but the skirt or dress would have pronounced her femininity. The difference is that women who want to be treated equally will opt for the masculine, but a woman that wants to be treated like a lady may choose femininity.

You may be asking, so what is feminine to us men? That's easy—everything that's the complete opposite of being a man. Yes, makeup and manicured nails are feminine, but ladies, the intangible things are what make us take notice and respect you for being a woman.

The way you sit, stand, walk and of course, talk, says a lot about you. We want to think about you and how you do that thing that we can't explain. You shouldn't be afraid to conquer at work, if you must. But again, when you get home, it's time to let your hair down and be a lady. We want it and believe me, we need it more than you know.

SEX APPEAL

So many women make the mistake that sex means sex appeal. It doesn't and we should note the difference.

Sex is an act that stems from the desire to share physical intimacy with another person. Having sex appeal is a whole other thing—and it doesn't always mean sex. A woman can be sexy by doing nothing at all. For some, simply standing there is sexy enough.

Dressing to provoke men to desire you for sex isn't sexy; it's tacky. If you disagree, try it and look at the kind of guys that approach you to see if they are long-term relationship types. Probably not.

But carrying yourself with confidence and class is sexy. It's not red carpet cleavage and sunglasses; it's what's behind the glasses that makes a woman sexy. No skin is needed to pull it off; being your true and intrinsic self will make you sexy beyond belief.

Don't believe the magazines; we men don't care if you have the latest trends in clothing or makeup. If you can capture our attention with a look, then you've got us. That's what the female mags are not telling you. There's a confidence that only a woman can exude that grips a man's heart and won't let go. He remembers it for years; well after he's moved on to other women. We never forget that one that caused us to tremble just from a look.

I remember seeing the way Michelle Obama looked at Barack the night he won the Presidency. Her eyes said it all. She was proud of him and proud of herself because they had achieved something together. At the end of the night, his walk carried the swagger that didn't just say, *hey, look at me, I just won the Presidency*, but it also said that his wife was his No. 1 fan.

Now that's sexy!

WHAT KEEPS A MAN ATTRACTED

Men love women that can keep them intrigued. Over time it's easy for a relationship to grow stale and a man can unconsciously lose focus. That can cause him to stray mentally. Any woman can continue to keep things energized with the right combination of mental and physical attraction.

As an entertainment development professional of many celebrity brands, my job included creating their looks and images, speaking skills and even the way they'd walk. Because of that ability I have been fortunate enough to garner some well-kept secrets that women of intrigue use to keep men emotionally and physically charged year after year.

Here are the basic things that are proven to attract men again and again over the years:

HEALTH CONSCIOUS

More than anything women must remember to get normal examinations. Breast cancer is no laughing matter; whether it runs in your family or not, the only way to ensure that you are safe is to get checked.

HEALTHY LIVING

The key to a well-groomed appearance is a healthy body. Eating healthy is the key. I can't explain it but there is something about healthy eating that seems feminine to men. It's a part of why we men don't like to do it ourselves. So when a woman does it, she appears feminine and she is staying healthy.

This doesn't mean being skinny or even thin. Personally, I love a woman with curves; so no matter what your body type remember that there is nothing more sexy than a woman that feels sexy in her own skin.

A daily dose of raw vegetables, fruits and non-processed foods is a great start to healthy living and don't forget that getting your man to join in will keep the playing field even.

FIT LIFESTYLE

Developing a fit lifestyle can keep a man on his toes. Ladies, many men are intimidated by a woman who is or gets fit. It's the illusion of attraction. You see, when a man has a fit woman, he thinks that more men will want her and if he isn't also looking the part, then the attention she receives may cause her to stray.

Women should use this to keep men engaged as well as to keep themselves active and healthy. A great way to start is to invite your mate to develop a fit lifestyle with you first, and if he resists, do your thing without him. Trust me, once he sees your body taking shape, the conqueror in him will kick in and he will join if for no other reason than to keep you looking at him.

RAISE YOUR STYLE IQ

"Dress for success" in every aspect of your life. Every woman should keep these basics in her closet; they never fail to keep a man interested.

Dress (classic skinny black dress never disappoints when you want a man's attention.)

Skirts (although women spend more time in pants today, every man loves a woman in a pencil skirt.)

Shirts (shirt styles are more unisex today, but men prefer women that know how to look like a lady. Nothing says feminine like a woman's blouse.)

Jeans (mixed with the right bag, a woman can pull off anything with a classic pair of good old faded blue jeans.)

Shoes (flats and sneakers are cool for kicking around, but a great pair of four-inch heels goes a long way with a guy.)

Swimwear (most men don't pay attention to the tassels, ruffles and ornaments on them. Guys love a classic bikini, and in your man's favorite color, you can't go wrong.)

Trends may come and go, but a man loves a woman that knows her stuff. You don't need to become a fashionista; using the basic essentials will always remind him of the perfect woman he has—classy and fun.

Fabrics

The fabrics that a woman wears say so much to a man. They can stimulate us mentally as well as physically and often refocus our attention to her at a moment's touch.

YES

Here are our favorites:

Cotton
(Keeps it simple and classic.)

Silk (Usually a blend of silk helps keep things cooler and men love the way it slides on a woman.)

Lycra
(It clings; you get my drift?)

Cashmere (It complements the softness of a woman.)

Leather (for that bad girl look)

Denim (There are no words for what it does to a woman's curves.)

NO

Fabrics to avoid:

Polyester (reserved for that '70s Halloween costume)

Rayon (If you have it, trade it in for cotton.)

100% wool (It chafes us.)

PATTERNS

Again, trends change from season to season, but the fact is that there is no replacing the basics on a woman. Basic black, white, pink, red, yellow and blue performed best with the men we asked. Lesser attractions were the more trendy plaids, sequins and young girl frilly ruffles. Men say they prefer a woman in the classics at almost all times.

LINGERIE AND UNDERGARMENTS

Brands don't matter much to men. It's all about the cut for us!

Thong (yes)
G-string (yes yes)
French cut (yes, yes, yes)
Boy shorts (Ooooooooooh yes)
No Granny panties! During those times of the month, women don't want to be sexy. And we men understand that during your cycle, you have a lot more to contend with than what kind of panties you should wear. But keep in mind that if you want us to picture you sexy, don't let us see you in the same "drawls" that our grandmothers wore. That ain't sexy!
Bras (Guys say they don't like to be fooled, so don't push up what you don't have…it's false advertisement.)

HAIR AND NAILS

It's impossible for men to say what they like for a woman's hair. Some men say they want it long; others like it shoulder-length. Then there are the guys that love the Halle Berry look, of course. The main thing is that it fits a woman's face and overall look.

The one thing that most men did agree on was that they preferred that a woman had her own style. They didn't go in for women with the latest reality show or singer's look. As long as a woman keeps it up, color didn't matter much to most guys, either. No, men don't prefer blondes; quite the opposite, you will find.

The larger concern was a woman's nails. Almost all the guys wanted a woman to get her hands and feet done at least once a month. And while nice nails were a must, natural nails were preferred over fake. "It takes too much time in the salon," one guy remarked and his sentiment seemed to be the consensus with most men.

If acrylic nails are your thing, then keep in mind that they are still supposed to look like they are your own nails. Men generally prefer a classy shape and French manicure. Long multi-colored nails are for women to take notice. If you want a man to keep looking, keep it classy!

This one actually goes for men and women—keep your feet up! C'mon, who wants to see some nasty corns, in-grown toenails or bunions? Nobody!

> **SIDE NOTE:**
> If getting a manicure and pedicure is out of reach, you can do it yourself at home with a simple nail kit. General upkeep goes a long way and with a little clipping, filing and polish, your nails can look as good as new.

BASIC NO-NOS

Never wear white pants or skirts with colored underwear…unless you want us to see them. Keep a pair of nudes in different styles for those days.

Never wear heels higher than four inches in the daytime (unless it's your work uniform).

Never wear fake leather; it looks like fake leather.

Don't dress for men; dress for your soul to be seen by one man.

Don't shave your unwanted facial or body hair, try waxing, threading or laser.

> **SIDE NOTE:**
> There are aberrations to every rule, so switch it up at your own discretion.

WHAT MEN LOVE TO HEAR

I recently had a conversation with a group of guys to find out what things they felt women should have. One of the last comments made was that "Women today talk like guys." I had to agree to an extent; society has meshed the roles of women and men and our dialects have also become the same.

Back in the day it was strange to hear a woman use the same words, inferences and slangs that a man used. Other women would look at her weird and she'd be told that to speak that way "isn't lady-like." But again, our reversal and collision of roles has changed that and women openly use many, if not all, of the same slang and inferences that men do in popular speech.

However, men miss those things that made women different than us. The soft and classy tone of a woman's voice on the phone sent chills up our spines once and we hunger for it now. It is the tone that soothes the savage beast in all of us. No matter how equal we become, we want to hear the whisper of femininity when it comes to our women.

So ladies, be secure in being 100 percent feminine. Yes, men want you to be our friends, but not talk like our buddies. Don't lose the things that remind us that you are a gift to our rough edges. That doesn't mean we want you to be frail; you can be strong and continue to elevate. But when you come home, allow us the opportunity to make you feel like a woman by reminding us that you are.

Sure, you should kick off your shoes and be comfortable in your relationship and in your home. But that doesn't include having a mouth like a sailor or a thug. Certain media want you to believe that all women talk like the females you see on the reality shows, but that isn't the case. A real woman knows who she is and expresses it in her speech.

Now, on the other hand, there is a time and place for everything and that also includes using foul language. Our mothers taught us that a lady should never curse, but I'm sure that didn't even apply to them in the bedroom. As adults we can technically speak how we want to, and curse words coming from a woman are the best in bed. It's the little touch that makes a good girl sound like a bad girl and it drives us out of our minds. Men agree on that one across the board!

> **SIDE NOTE:**
> Never use curse words in an argument with a man. It makes you his adversary and he will always try to conquer an adversary.

THE TRUTH ABOUT MEN AND DOMESTIC WOMEN

Recently I was at a friend's gathering where the attendees were split 50% male, and 50% female; all of whom were working and college educated.

During the post-dinner conversation we somehow got engaged in a discussion about performing domestic duties. The interesting thing was that all of the women seemed to feel like being domestic was no longer needed because they had professional careers. But the men, who were also professionals, felt that they should perform at least some domestic duties within the home.

Whatever happened to the pride that women felt from performing duties like cleaning, cooking or doing laundry? How did this become so beneath the modern woman? Most guys like this quality in a woman and say they are more inclined to choose a woman that has domestic attributes.

To see how women really felt about this issue, I polled ten professional women between the ages of twenty-four to thirty-five to see how many of them had learned basic domestic attributes. The numbers were shocking; only two out of ten could actually cook. And of that same group, only four out of ten even wanted to learn if it was made available to them, but they weren't going to pursue it on their own.

These modern women seem to have grown up in a world where their parents neglected to teach them that domesticity is a gift, not a chore. Their new intellectually advanced prowess gave them the idea that cooking or cleaning for a home was demeaning. One of them remarked that she could afford for she and her man to eat out. But she didn't realize is that if a woman wants to keep a good man, he will want to eat from his woman's own hands at some point.

We men know that women also go to work just like us, so we should also learn domestic duties. But our work schedules don't mean we should be eating from burger or taco stands, instead of our women's hands. Believe me, there is nothing more pleasurable than the feeling a man or kids get after eating from their mother's kitchen.

Especially because our mothers knew how to work and cook, we have the natural desire for our women to be able to do what Mom did.

Being domestic is not like being sentenced to the dungeon, so please don't take offense to man's expectation of female domesticity. If you still want to keep the attitude that domesticity is beneath you, then it's completely your decision. But don't get mad if that doesn't bring you great results in your relationship; here you have the real information that you need to have a happy and committed modern man.

So ladies, forget the old way of thinking. Both men and women should work to be well rounded and here are some basic domestic essentials that will help you to maintain a more complete relationship:

- Doing laundry
- Ironing clothes
- Making the bed
- Vacuuming
- Cooking

MAKING IT FUN

Last, and most importantly, is that we men want to have fun with our mates. Guys complain that once they are in a committed relationship with a woman, the fun stops. Keeping a man in good spirits makes a happy relationship, so you've gotta have fun with him, no matter what. If not he'll want to flee and watch all the games with his boys, and that isn't healthy for the relationship.

Learn the things he likes and take an interest in them. He'll love and respect you for it and it gives you more time together.

TO BE CONTINUED...

Make It Fun Together

Men love to go panty shopping. It makes us anticipate what we're going to get at the end of the day.

Don't be afraid to be a bad girl. Invite your man to a strip club or take a pole-dancing class. Trust me, we can't wait to see what you've learned.

Send him texts and email photos of you, for no reason, with enticing messages.

Instead of asking him to take you out offer him to stay in and have dinner on you.

Try a "whatever you like night"— you may be surprised to see that he just wants to be with you.

You may not believe it, but men aren't always thinking about sex. Buy tickets to his favorite thing to do and go with him.

About the Authors

MAXWELL BILLIEON

Maxwell Billieon was born into a family deeply rooted in social and political affairs. A true renaissance man, the multilingual native Californian found his earliest influences in family members who held the political offices of Congressman, Senator and Lieutenant Governor; as well as members of the professional sports and entertainment industries. Their examples provided Billieon with the blueprints he would need to travel the globe, building a life less ordinary.

In his youth, Billieon excelled as an athlete and in the performance arts, also building a reputation for being a dapper dresser. During his collegiate years, Billieon majored in International Business and as fate would have it, a rare encounter with a celebrity artist gave Billieon the opportunity to leave college and tour the world as choreographer/creative director. He accepted and went on to develop celebrity talents that garnered over $100 million in global sales. That success enabled Billieon to open his own entertainment corporation, which he partnered with a major music distributor.

Always on the cutting edge, it didn't take long before Billieon began to venture into other arenas; and in 2006, launching his namesake corporation, The Billieon Group (TBG), Billieon began the development of high-end luxury lifestyle goods and accessories that are now sold globally. This diversity garnered Billieon the moniker, "The Lifestyle Guru."

Alongside his professional success, Billieon directed his attention toward the advancement of at-risk communities as a public speaker to colleges, corporations, government and various non-profit and philanthropic organizations. Billieon also became an orator for the U.S. National Legislative Black Caucus (foundation), adding another star to his array of accomplishments. But of all of Billieon's extraordinary achievements, it is his personal reformation from *Cheating Man* that he is most proud of.

In his youth, Billieon learned that most men cheat in relationships. Consequently, Billieon cheated non-stop from his adolescent years, until he was thirty-two years old. It was then, in what Billieon refers to as the age of intellectualism, that he began his search to learn *how not to cheat*. With no mentors to be found, Billieon crafted his own escape from the trappings of infidelity, via the development of what he has coined as the "Six Virtues of a New Man." These virtues led Billieon, and the countless other men and women that have followed them, to having faithful, "monogamy capable" relationships.

Now, as the premier boisterous and outspoken guru on the subject of cheating, Billieon has become a consultant to the U.S. military on soldier relationships and he is well-respected by many celebrities, athletes and politicians for developing the principles that help them deal with the challenges of infidelity they face.

Billieon believes that "cheating is causing the demise of the human family," and with this as his inspiration for change, Billieon has a host of Internet and social network portals to teacch others.

Book Info: DeathOfTheCheatingMan.com
Personal info and speaking: MaxwellBillieon.com
Videos: Youtube.com/MakingTheNewMan
Social Media: twitter.com/MaxwellBillieon; twitter.com/MakingTheNewMan; twitter.com/DeathOfTheCheatingMan

Utilizing his experiences as well as the facts that both men and women need to hear, Maxwell Billieon is on a mission to enhance relationships by putting an end to cheating forever.

RAY J

Television show personality and multi-platinum music artist Ray J became a household name at a young age. Early success in commercials, television shows and movies garnered him a recording deal and before he knew it, he was a budding celebrity.

After his very public and infamous relationship with Kim K, everyone wanted to know more about his relationships with a bevy of other beautiful models, singers and actresses, making pop culture headlines all over the world. His playboy persona spawned the hit television show, *For the Love of Ray J*, and the spin-off, *Brandy & Ray J—A Family Business;* with Ray J as Executive Producer, both shows went to No. 1 on the VH1 network, showcasing his anything-goes, cheating lifestyle.

That success accompanied his top ten albums, *Raydiation* and *All I Feel*, on Ray J's own Knockout music label. His discography also boasts a list of countless smash singles on the pop, R&B and urban charts and he has several guest appearances with the music industry's elite artists. In addition, Ray J's national appearances on *Jay Leno*, *Regis & Kelly*, *Good Morning America*, *George Lopez*, *Wendy Williams* and a host of other top shows, have all helped make him one of the web's top trending personalities with millions of adoring female fans worldwide.

What no one ever knew was that for many years, Ray J lived a secret life of cheating. In *Death of the Cheating Man*, Ray J sets out on a journey to put his cheating on women to an end. He finds the perfect teacher in cheating expert and relationship guru, Maxwell Billieon. Along the road to learning *how not to cheat*, Ray J comes clean about his secret cheating life, revealing his most intimate stories, as he learns the virtues he needs to change his cheating ways and become a new man forever.

Ray J's affiliated social media networks include:
www.rayj.com
www.twitter.com/rayj

Just the Facts: Q & A

What is cheating?

The breaking of any rule that governs a couple's intimate relationships or interactions with other people.

Why do men cheat?

Because we have not been taught "how not to cheat!" We have never been given the six basic principles of learning how not to cheat.

Do all men cheat?

No—many men have learned and mastered the six principles of learning how not to cheat.

What percentage of men cheat in relationships?

57 percent

What are the six basic principles of learning how not to cheat?

- Developing an internal voice
- Establishing a consequence mechanism
- Building self-restraint
- Knowing your limitations
- Being honest with yourself
- Becoming a thinking man

What is "The New Monogamy"?

Each couple now has the ability to make its own rules to fit its individually jointed relationships.

Where can I learn more or see the author speak about cheating?

www.MakingTheNewMan.com
www.youtube.com/makingthenewman
www.DeathOfTheCheatingMan.com
www.MaxwellBillieon.com
www.RayJ.com

For bookings, public speaking and appearances, where can I contact the author?

bookings@deathofthecheatingman.com
bookings@makingthenewman.com
bookings@maxwellbillieon.com
bookings@thebillieongroup.com

Reader's Discussion Guide

Join the cheating discussion by asking your friends, family, book club or even yourself the following questions.

1) Have you ever cheated?

2) Have you ever been cheated on and if so, how did you find out?

3) Have you ever confronted a cheating mate?

4) Do you believe that men can "learn how not to cheat?"

5) Do you believe that men have any reasons to cheat; if so, what are they?

6) Is it worse for a man to cheat on his spouse than it is to cheat on his girlfriend?

7) Why do you think men cheat?

8) Why do you think men cheat more than women?

9) Do you think that schools should teach young males courses on relationships, monogamy and cheating?

10) Do you think that male cheating causes female cheating?

11) Should cheating be illegal or against the law; if so, what should the penalty be?

12) Do you believe that society should move toward a more consequence-based system of behavior?